MW01592865

MORE EQUAL THAN OTHERS
A STUDY OF THE INDIAN LEFT

MORE EQUAL THAN OTHERS

A STUDY OF THE INDIAN LEFT

Ravi Shanker Kapoor

VISION BOOKS

(Incorporating Orient Paperbacks)

This book is dedicated to
my elder brother,
Late Shri Gouri Shanker Kapoor

ISBN 81-7094-381-7

© Ravi Shanker Kapoor, 2000

First Published in 2000 by
Vision Books Pvt. Ltd.
(Incorporating Orient Paperbacks & CARING imprints)
24 Feroze Gandhi Road, Lajpat Nagar III
New Delhi-110024 (India)
Phone: (+91-11) 6836470; 80
Fax: (+91-11) 6836490
E-mail: visionbk@vsnl.com

Printed at
Rashtra Rachna Printers
C-88, Ganesh Nagar, Pandav Nagar Complex,
Delhi-110092 (India).

Contents

Acknowledgments

IT WAS DURING DISCUSSIONS WITH MY FRIENDS VIBHAY JHA and Bhashyam Kasturi that the idea to write this book was born. Extensive interaction with Kapil Malhotra and Bhawesh Mishra enriched the text. Discussions with Sudhish Pachauri, Swapan Dasgupta, Uma Shanker Pathik, Sushant Sareen, Soumitra Mohan, and Soumya Sarkar helped cut down flab and make the book more focused. The expertise of Kamal Khanna in computers made my job convenient. Without the encouragement from my niece Deepti, nephew Aditya, *bhabhi* Sukhwant Kapoor, and all my friends, the completion of the book would have been impossible.

Introduction

WHY SHOULD YOU READ THIS BOOK ON THE INDIAN Left? Or, for that matter, *any* book on the Indian Left? After all, Leftist parties are suffering a decline; during the nineties their strength in Parliament was not even 10 per cent. The Left may not be following in the footsteps of dinosaurs, but it hardly seems to be a force to reckon with any more so far as electoral arithmetic is concerned. So, why did I spend so much time on the Left writing this book, and why should the reader spend some of his?

The Left has to be studied if we are interested in understanding the trends and forces determining the shape of contemporary India in a comprehensive manner; for, the *influence* of the Left is greatly disproportionate to its actual political and electoral *strength*.

This brings us back to the first question: why this book? The answer is: because all other accounts of the Left leave a lot to be desired. There are two kinds of writings on the Left. One is the sympathetic writings — by the Left, for the Left, and of the Left — either laudatory accounts or friendly criticism. Another genre is vituperative literature whose assertions have become trite, stale, and inconsequential: communists were the lackeys of Moscow and Beijing; they betrayed the country in 1942; they supported the two-nation theory of the Muslim League, they are the orphaned children of Marx, and so on. I have tried to avoid the extremes as well as the trite. Therefore, I have not written much on the role of the communists in the Quit India movement in 1942, although I have touched upon the issue.

Often the failings of Indian communists have been explained in terms of their excessive dependence on Moscow or Beijing. I feel that this dependence was not as much a cause as a consequence — a consequence of their rootlessness. This seems to be a startling assertion. For, communists claim to be the champions of the masses, the downtrodden, the subalterns, the people. But the masses, as the Indian communists see them, are bereft of any social and cultural content; they are innocent, inherently good and noble, without any caste bias, religious prejudice, or parochial feelings; they are mere abstractions. They are not the people you and I come across every day. To understand the *real* masses, one has to identify oneself with the masses; at least, one should be able to empathize with them. Indian communists were not able to do that, thanks to the British legacy which made them intellectually and temperamentally un-Indian.

Macaulay, the great imperialist, was of the opinion that the British should "form a class who may be interpreters between us and the millions we govern; a class of persons, Indian in blood and color, but British in taste, in opinion, in morals, and in intellect." The Indian Communists were the most consistent and earnest Macaulayns. They viewed the history, society, culture, and traditions of India as a European would do. At the heart of their rootlessness were two factors: the push factor, i.e., the Macaulayan syndrome; and the pull factor, i.e., the internationalism and abstractions of Marxism. The pull factor did away with whatever Indianness was left in the communist leaders. Hence their escape from concrete realities to abstract fantasies, from nation to ideology. A natural corollary was an abject surrender to the diktats of Moscow. For, who else can interpret the ideology better than those who had successfully implemented it?

I have focused not only on the political history of the Left but also its role in other spheres of life like art, culture, literature, education and cinema. I feel that the Left's tremendous influence and its intellectual hegemony can never be properly understood without analyzing its involvement in these areas. In fact, intellectual hegemony of the Left is the main thesis that I have propounded in the book; and it was this hegemony that prompted me to write it. This hegemony did not come to me as a revelation; it was over the years that I could get some grasp on the genesis, anatomy, and dynamics of this hegemony.

I first became aware of the Left's hegemony and its proximity to the Establishment, in the early eighties, when I saw Govind Nihalani's *Akrosh*. The movie denounced the apathy of the middle class and depicted the struggle of radicals against the ruthless exploitation of tribals. I must admit that the movie had an impact on me. I had just passed out of my school and was under the influence of Leftist ideas and ideals, though I was never a member of any of the student wings of the various communist parties. But I also learnt that the movie was financed by National Film Development Corporation and awarded by the government. I found this curious and inscrutable — how was it that the system was sponsoring something which apparently sought to undermine it?

In early 1985, I visited Jawaharlal Nehru University (JNU) for the first time; I was then studying at Hansraj College of Delhi University. The country had gone though a general election a few months back. There were many slogans on the walls of the campus, of which one I remember one: "Revolution is the festival of the masses/Election is the festival of the asses". The JNU visit raised another set of questions in my mind: Why was the government providing all sorts of facilities to this university which was a hotbed of various kinds revolutionary ideas? Interestingly, it was not only the students who were known for their radicalism but also a number of teachers. And the university was taken care of very well — it had a sprawling campus, decent hostel facilities for most students, and a well-maintained library. The other universities in the country are in terrible shape by comparison; even Delhi University, looked like poor cousins of JNU as far as facilities were concerned. So why was JNU pampered? Why was the state so hard-bent on promoting subversive elements? Or were they really subversives, for many JNU dons were authorities in different branches of knowledge?

Another incident I clearly remember was the aftermath of Bharatiya Janata Party president Lal Krishna Advani's arrest in Bihar in 1990. He was leading the famous *Rathyatra* from Somnath to Ayodhya. Those were interesting times: Prime Minister VP Singh had unleashed the Mandal monster; there were demonstrations everywhere in north India and young people had immolated themselves; with the movement for Ram temple gaining momentum, *kar sevaks* in UP were fired upon by the police, resulting in a number of casualties; in general, the political climate was charged up. It was in this atmosphere that Doordarshan organized a programme in which many "intellectuals" commented upon the Ramjanmabhoomi-Babri Masjid issue. Two things infuriated me. One was the fact that film actors Dilip Kumar and Raj Babbar were among those "intellectuals." I wondered how they counted as intellectuals. Was it because they conformed to a certain pattern of thinking? The second, and this was the most conspicuous feature of the entire programme, was the absence of even any semblance of dissent. Everybody was saying the same thing: the BJP is fanning communal feelings; the Ram temple movement is anti-national, unethical, etc; why can't the BJP build the temple at some other place; why can't a temple and a mosque co-exist; and so on. I was against the BJP's temple movement, but the excesses of secularists disgusted me. Why weren't they allowing the other party at least to put up its case?

This reminds me of the disenchantment of one of my friends with the Hindutva cause. He comes from a family which is a strong supporter of the RSS. Many of the family members have been attending RSS *shakhas* since decades. He himself studied in a school run by the RSS. While in school, he once participated in a tour of historical places. At one of the monuments they visited, there was a grave of a Muslim ruler. One of the students, whose heart was full of anger for the depredations of Muslim rulers during the medieval period, threw a banana peel at the grave. The teacher accompanying the boys patted the back of the boy who had desecrated the grave. From that day, my friend ceased to be an active member of the RSS (though he still votes for the BJP). In my case, too, I feel it was the excess of secular rhetoric which made me rethink about politics.

During the Ram temple movement almost all intellectuals — historians, artists, writers, journalists, academics — campaigned against the BJP. They were Leftists of various hues. And when the Safdar Hashmi Memorial Trust (Sahmat) started its antics, the intellectual class supported it. So did the government: Sahmat soon became a pampered child of the authorities. Why was the state promoting an essentially Leftist outfit which was, or pretended to be, anti-Establishment? I started looking for answers.

This was also the period in which Mandalization had become a fact of Indian politics. VP Singh is generally remembered for his decision to implement the Mandal Commission's recommendations. His equally — if not more — important contribution has gone unnoticed: he played a key role in bringing together the two streams of the Indian Left, the communists and the socialists. Often the latter are ignored in any discourse on the Indian Left, but I feel that the importance of socialists in independent India can hardly be overemphasized. Thus, I have comprehensively dealt with the love-hate relationship between the communists and the socialists.

The book, I would like to think, is also comprehensive on another count. I have not restricted myself to political issues; I have discussed extensively art, culture, cinema, literature, etc. I believe that no work on the Indian Leftists would be complete without taking into account their tremendous influence on these areas.

CHAPTER 1

The Left Is Always Right

Where Hypocrisy Is the Creed

Consistency, they say, is the virtue of asses. West Bengal Chief Minister Jyoti Basu, being a leader of the masses, is certainly not enamored of such a bourgeois virtue. Therefore, the leader of the Communist Party of India (Marxist), did not feel any qualms about uprooting thousands of hawkers and rendering them jobless in Calcutta towards the end of 1996. His trusted comrade, Subhash Chakravorty, who was in charge of cleaning up the city, saw to it that the operation was done with ruthless efficiency.

.The idea was to attract international capital to West Bengal. The mess the hawkers had made of the city streets could have dampened the investing enthusiasm of the 2,500-strong business delegation that accompanied British Prime Minister John Major. The occasion was the CII Partnership Summit '97 in January.

Basu made his intentions amply clear. He told the gathering of Indian and British industrialists quite candidly that "the color of the government is not important" as far as economic matters are concerned. And for such candor and market-friendliness, he was commended by the well-known tycoon, Swraj Paul. "He is the greatest chief minister India has ever had". It is not very often that one comes across such fulsome praise of a communist by a capitalist, even in the post-Cold War era.

There were three unusual features in the entire episode. First, the Marxist government's ruthless attitude towards the subalterns — in this case, the hawkers. Second, the communists' wooing of the capitalists. But the most conspicuous feature was the lukewarm reaction of the otherwise voluble Leftist, progressive intellectuals. Shamsul Islam, a Marxist who does theater, wrote in the *Navbharat Times* (2 February 1997): "It seemed as if all eminent people had had a tacit understanding. Though Calcutta's progressive writers and artists did issue a statement [regarding the removal of hawkers], even that statement could not condemn the government action."

This is not to suggest that the removal of hawkers should have been condemned by all. After all, those who encroach on government land — whether they are hawkers or squatters — cannot expect to be treated with kid gloves. The morality of the action is not the moot point. But consider a hypothetical scenario: had a similar exercise been carried out by the Digvijay Singh government in Bhopal or the Bhairon Singh Shekhawat government in Jaipur, all hell would have been let loose by Leftists of all hues. There would have been protest marches in Delhi, Bombay, and other cities; angry letters to newspaper editors; seminars lambasting the "anti-poor" drives; a deluge of words. A fact-finding team would have been sent from, where else but, Jawaharlal Nehru University of the capital. Earth-shaking rhetoric would have erupted like lava — "the comprador class has sold the country", "a sickening assault on the have-nots", "the fascist forces have been exposed", and what have you. However, there was no bang, not even a whimper; what followed was a thundering silence or, as Islam put it, "a tacit understanding" among the Leftist intellectuals.

The moral of the story is: the Left is always right and the others always wrong.

If PV Narasimha Rao liberalizes the economy, he is favoring the captains of industry; if Jyoti Basu does something similar, he is promoting industrialization in the state. If Manmohan Singh invites foreign capital, he is compromising the economic sovereignty of the country; if Somnath Chatterjee, Chairman,

West Bengal Industrial Development Corporation, does the same, he is working hard to reduce unemployment.

The we-are-always-right-and-the-others-always-wrong syndrome of Leftists is not confined to the economic arena; it is evident in other spheres also. Take, for instance, the Miss World 96 contest that was held in Bangalore. Brinda Karat, General Secretary of the All India Democratic Women's Association (AIDWA), the women's wing of the CPM, wrote in a newsmagazine, *The Frontline*, that "the contest was an insult to the vast masses of India's women." Subhasini Ali, Joint Secretary of AIDWA, told an interviewer of the same magazine that the pageant "represents an exploitative culture that is based on the commercialization of social relations."

Ironically, these ladies were as critical of the organizers of the beauty contest as they were of the women activists of the Bharatiya Janata Party (BJP) who were also protesting against the show. According to Karat, the BJP's interpretation of Indian culture is "for the subordination of women." In other words, if the Leftists oppose beauty contests, their protest is against the alleged "commodification of women"; if the Rightists do the same, they are working on an anti-women agenda.

The CPM leaders and sympathizer-intellectuals never tire of condemning the rise of consumerism, but do not find anything wrong if the party organ, *Ganashakti*, carries an advertisement of Coca Cola — the product which often symbolized neo-imperialism in Leftist parlance (remember the term Coca Colonization?).

Let's go back in history. Mahatma Gandhi, Congress Socialists, and other Congress leaders vacillated for some time regarding their stand on the issue of World War II. The communists thundered: "No longer is Gandhiji's leadership, in even a restricted sense, a unifier of the people's movement, no longer has it any progressive role whatsoever. Compromise on the issue of the war [that is, not opposing the 'imperialist war'] is the biggest danger that faces the national movement and Gandhism today means the line of compromise." Further, "the CSP (Congress Socialist Party) leadership has made its final break with Marxism and has completely gone over to Gandhism." But when the Soviet Union was attacked by Hitler and the "imperialist war" metamorphosed into a "People's War," the Indian freedom fighters became "fifth columnists" and "traitors" whom the people should "treat as the worst enemy of the nation." In short, the communists were right when they were opposing the British government, and equally they were right when they were supporting it!

If the EMS Namboodiripad government in Kerala is dismissed by New Delhi, it is an assault on the federal structure of our polity; if the BJP government in UP is dismissed, it is an effort to check communal forces. If the BJP or the Congress ally with corrupt politicians, it's the height of immorality; if the Left befriends similar characters, it is in the interests of the people. If the CPI(M) allies with the Muslim League, it is in the interest of the subalterns; but if the Congress does the same, it is an opportunistic alliance. If the BJP sponsors rewriting of history, it is an exercise in deceitfulness, distortion, and prevarication; but if the Leftist historians do the same — as they have been doing, the NCERT textbooks being an example — it is putting history in proper perspective.

When Chandrashekhar, a leader of the Communist Party of India (Marxist-Leninist) at the Delhi-based Jawaharlal Nehru University, was murdered in Bihar in 1997, he was equated with Bhagat Singh, Sukhdev, and Rajguru. Chandrashekhar was hailed as "the young revolutionary who died on the street defending his ideals, chasing a dream, not only for himself, but others as well." These were the words commemorating the CPI(ML) leader on his first death anniversary in *The Pioneer*. In the same paper, it was pointed out that while the Leftists of all hues were solemnly talking about the loss of Chandrashekhar, they did not even bother to mourn the gruesome murder of another student leader, Paramsivam, in Tamil Nadu. Paramsivam was hacked to death. Was this apathy because Paramsivam belonged to the Akhil Bharatiya Vidyarthi Parishad, the student wing of the Sangh Parivar?

There are any number of such examples of the duplicity and double-speak of the Indian Leftists. Yet, they are seldom derided or criticized for their duplicity. Their cranky theories pass off as self-evident truths; their propaganda, as well-established facts. The reason is the tremendous intellectual hegemony they enjoy in the media, academic circles, and the opinion-making apparatus in the country.

Intellectual Hegemony of the Left (1)

In the wake of the demolition of the Babri Masjid on 6 December 1992, pro-BJP writers used the term "Left-wing McCarthyism" for the aggression with which Hindu nationalism was berated and denigrated. However, one feels that it is not a very appropriate term to describe the Left's stranglehold over the intellectual class.

For one, the era characterized by the US Senator Joseph McCarthy (1908-57) did not last more than five years. He shot into prominence in February 1950 when he alleged that 205 communists had infiltrated the State Department; after his censure in the Senate on 2 December 1954, for conduct "contrary to Senate traditions," he passed into oblivion. Second, McCarthyism was essentially political in nature. However, what India has witnessed is something more enduring, widespread (read ubiquitous), and inveterate.

It must be noted that the credibility of communists had suffered tremendously due to their traitorous role during the People's War phase. Even a socialist like Jawaharlal Nehru accused them of betraying the nation at a crucial juncture. Therefore, it is amazing that the communists and fellow-travelers gained legitimacy and recognition just a few years after Independence which they had declared as fake. Let's see how it happened.

Communism in India (1960), written by Gene D Overstreet and Marshall Windmiller, discusses at length the activities of the Left and how it spread its influence over the intelligentsia. The book "was written under the auspices of the Modern India

Project at the University of California, Berkeley. . . . Financial support for the efforts of the project was granted by the Ford Foundation," which makes it vulnerable against communist attack; it can easily be dismissed by the comrades as a routine Cold War exercise of the American imperialists. However, this book is a useful source of information, and the veracity of the facts cannot be challenged even by the most dogmatic communist. Chapter XVII, "Fronts and Fellow Travelers", is particularly germane to our area of interest.

"Just as the mass organizations (like the students, workers, and women wings of communist parties) serve as 'transmission belts' between the Party and the working class at large, so 'front' organizations link the Party to 'progressive' elements of other classes," wrote Overstreet and Windmiller. The origins of communist fronts can "probably be credited to Willie Munzenburg," a German communist. He also founded "the League Against Imperialism" which from 1927 to 1931 could boast of the presence of Jawaharlal Nehru on its executive committee.

Since World War II Communist fronts have appeared in India in abundance. In accordance with the policy established in the Comintern as early as 1926, there has been created "a whole solar system of organizations and smaller committees around the Communist party, so to speak, smaller organizations working actually under the influence of one party."

These fronts serve two primary purposes. As propaganda forums, they help to create a climate of public opinion favorable to party activities, and as sources of recruitment they provide a sphere where political activists of all sorts can be observed, influenced, and drawn into the party apparatus.

These fronts could be used for communist propaganda without losing the veneer of objectivity. Later, they become not just recruitment centers but also platforms for the ambitious and the fraudulent to hobnob with prominent personalities in various fields. Communists were always keen to involve established figures in their own right. So, it was "with the blessings of

Rabindranath Tagore" that the Bengal Friends of the Soviet Union was organized in 1941. "The organization became national when on 3 and 4 June 1944, the first Congress of the All-India Friends of the Soviet Union was held at Bombay University's Convention Hall. Approximately 2,000 people from all parts of India attended the meeting, 100 of them being delegates. The affair was a huge success in terms of non-Communist personalities who had been induced to participate." They included Sarojini Naidu, Vijayalakshmi Pandit, Syed Abdulla Brelvi, Mahakavi Vallathol, the Malabar poet who was to become a "permanent fixture in Communist fronts", and Bhupendranath Datta, one of the members of Virendranath Chattopadhyaya's delegation to the third Comintern Congress.

In the fifties, another forum to air pro-Soviet views was the World Peace Movement. According to Overstreet and Windmiller: "Of all Communist fronts in India, the most elaborate and most effective have been the various organizations set up to advance the theme that the Soviet Union is the leading champion of world peace." A galaxy of luminaries from various spheres of life adorned this movement were the mathematician-historian DD Koshambi — litterateurs like Mulk Raj Anand, Krishan Chander, Mahakavi Vallathol, Ali Sardar Jafri, Sardar Gurbax Singh, Khwaja Ahmed Abbas, and Indulal Yagnik; RK Karanjia, editor of the *Blitz*; Prithvi Raj Kapoor, a leading film personality; Dr. JC Kumarappa, a "Gandhian economist", freedom fighters like Saifudin Kitchlew; and intellectuals like Romesh and Raj Thapar.

On similar lines, the Indo-China Friendship Association was formed. Those promoting Sino-Indian ties included RK Karanjia, Aruna Asaf Ali, a well-connected Leftist and freedom fighter, Dr. VKRV Rao, Director, Delhi School of Economics, Dr. Gyan Chand, former chief of the Financial Division of the International Monetary Fund, Mulk Raj Anand, Saifudin Kitchlew, Gurbax Singh, Chaudhry Brahm Prakash, Chief Minister of Delhi State, and KM Panikkar, a former ambassador to China.

Many other pro-communist bodies were also formed. Several progressive writers' associations were organized in which eminent people like Mulk Raj Anand, Munshi Premchand, Sarojini Naidu, Krishan Chander, KA Abbas, Shivdan Singh Chauhan, Ramananda Chatterjee and Ram Bilas Sharma participated. Over the decades, the progressive movement became the strongest influence in Hindi literature. In fact, the list of progressive writers reads like the who's who of litterateurs.

According to *A History of Indian Literature: 1911-56*, written by Sisir Kumar Das and brought out by the Sahitya Akademi:

> One of the significant events in the history of modern Indian literature is the formation of the All India Progressive Writers' Association (AIPWA). . . AIPWA held its first meeting in Lucknow in 1936 under the presidentship of Premchand.

Premchand was the "first major Indian writer to respond to Marxism and socialism as an alternative to Gandhian politics." He opined, "To hope that the capitalists will desist from exploiting the helpless condition of the peasants is like expecting a dog to stand watch over a piece of meat," which debunks the Gandhian theory of trusteeship.

Das traces the AIPWA's history:

> This [Lucknow] meeting was a culmination of moods, efforts and initiatives that began with the publication of *Angare* (1932), a collection of ten works, including five stories by Sajjad Zaheer (who later became a prominent leader of the CPI), all written in Urdu and extremely radical in temperament. Sajjad Zaheer (1905-73) during his stay in London as a student was exposed to Marxism. He met several leftist writers, including Ralph Fox (1900-37), whose *The Novel and the People* became popular among the Marxists. During a conversation with Fox the idea of a Progressive Writers' Association was mooted. A draft was prepared by Mulk Raj Anand. An edited version of it appeared in the *Left Review* (London) in February 1935 and a revised version in Hindi was published in the October 1935 issue of *Hans*, edited by Premchand.

The second phase of the pre-history of AIPWA is the meeting of writers in Paris in June 1935. It was the International Congress of Writers, organized by Andre Gide, Henri Barbusse, Romain Rolland and Andre Malraux. . . . Sajjad Zaheer and Mulk Raj Anand were the two Indian writers to be present in the meeting attended by galaxy of European writers. . . .

The conference encouraged Zaheer farther towards his mission to form the Progressive Writers' Association in India. . . .

Although the Association was technically not the forum of any political group, and it certainly was formed with the intention to provide a broad platform to all writers sharing certain common values, slowly it came to be identified with the Marxists.

In the field of theater, too, the Leftist influence was perceptible from the forties. The Indian People's Theater Association (IPTA), was formed in 1943. Writes Sisir Kumar Das:

It is not very clear whether IPTA was formed under a directive of the Communist Party of India or it grew out of the general temper of resistance against fascism and enthusiastic response to socialism. Although it meant to serve the common man IPTA was dominated by intellectuals and in the formative stage its impact was rather limited. . . .

The [Bengal] famine and the [Second World] war and the final stage of the political struggle, and the exposure to Marxism as well as to the Western dramatic techniques all exerted influence on the theater. However, Khwaja Abbas informs that an IPTA performance in Bangalore was given before 600 mill workers and they responded warmly. The early plays were propagandist and didactic, directed to the cause of trade union. The first major contribution of the IPTA was the production of *Nabanna* (1944, *The New Rice*) by Bijan Bhattacharya. . . . The IPTA started with a dance drama, *Hunger and Epidemic*, on the Bengal famine. Its powerful depiction of the famine, which was soon followed by Bijan Bhattacharya's one-act play *Jabanbandi* (1943) and then by

Nabanna directed by the legendary actor Sambhu Mitra created history.

The famine and the war and the final stage of the political struggle, and the exposure to Marxism as well as to the Western dramatic techniques all exerted influence on the theater. . . . A large number of plays were written in various languages foregrounding the common man, the exploited man in particular, and the tension between the landlord and the peasant and the tug of war between the industrialist and the laborer. The trend started even before the Progressive Writers' meet but it was intensified after it. . . . K Damodaran (1912-76), for example, wrote a play entitled *Pattabakki* (Rental Arrears) in 1938. It was performed as a part of the political movement to organize the landless agricultural laborers. The play demanded the immediate replacement of feudal economic system by a socialist system. *Pattabakki*, the first political play in Malayalam, encouraged many dramatists. . .

Another writer, Thoppil Bhasi. . . also a communist, wrote several plays which were repeatedly performed by the Kerala People Arts Club. One of his famous plays is *Ninnal Enne Communistakki* (You have made me a communist, 1952). The new wave also touched Punjabi drama which entered into a new phase of its history with the one-act plays of Sant Singh Sekhon, and plays of Gurdial Singh Khosla and particularly those of Balwant Gargi, who laid the foundations of a professional theater in Punjab. Gargi came under the spell of the progressive movement. . . . The progressive movement created a new space for the dramatist to express himself with greater freedom; not only did he write "committed" plays, but also experimented with the areas of human emotions often neglected by earlier dramatists. . . .

In Andhra Pradesh, IPTA exploited the folk forms, particularly the *burra katha*, *harikatha*; as they used *powda* in Maharashtra. . . .

In 1947 the Telugu Little Theater was founded by K Subba Rao at Bezwada, on the model of the Little Theater movement in England. That very year Utpal Datta (1929-93), also a member of the IPTA and involved with English language theater, who had training with Geoffrey Kendal's *Shakespeariana*, formed his own troupe Little Theater Group. The Communists Party of India, like the DMK, realized the power of the stage in the propagation of political ideology and used theater very effectively. "Kerala Peoples Art Club" in Trivandrum staged a play entitled *Ninnal Enne Communistakki* (You have made me a communist) in 1952 for more than 600 times.

This is also the time of the apprenticeship of several significant dramatists who dominated the Indian theater in the coming decades. The Oriya playwright Manoranjan Das's plays, *Agami* (1950), and *Buxi Jagabadhu* (1951) and Vijay Tendulkar's *Manas Navace Bet* (An island called Man, 1956) appeared during this period. They matured in the next decade with Badal Sarkar (b 1925), Mohan Rakesh (1925-72), Girish Karnad (b 1938) and Cho S Ramaswamy (b 1934).

The fact that the Marxist influence on Indian theater has been profound and pronounced can hardly be over-emphasized. In the social, economic, and political conditions of that period, it was not unnatural for playwrights to be attracted towards communism. And the CPI capitalized on this. IPTA may or may not have been founded by the CPI, but it was definitely used by the party to further the party interests.

On the lines of the AIPWA and IPTA, the All India Association of Democratic Lawyers was also formed, though it did not play as important a role as other communist organizations did.

Such was the state of affairs in the 1950s. The environment was conducive to such activities. For one, there was the euphoria of newly-found freedom, boundless enthusiasm to build a new India, a deeply-felt concern to remove inequalities in the society. Most of the people mentioned above and many other intellectuals genuinely believed that socialism was the panacea for all ills mankind was afflicted with.

The political background, too, was favorable. On the one hand was Anglo-American imperialism — and the intelligentsia in a newly-liberated colony could hardly be expected to be favorably disposed towards the Western bloc. On the other hand, there was the Soviet Union, which was sympathetic towards nations fighting against Western hegemony. Hence Afro-Asian solidarity, thirdworldism, non-alignment, and other such temptations and curiosities. Further, the Nehru government's foreign policy was more or less tilted towards the Soviet Union and China. Moscow often advised the Communist Party of India to appreciate Nehru's progressive role in shaping the nation.

This is not to suggest that all fellow-travelers and other Leftist intellectuals were totally mesmerized by Nehru or turned a blind eye to the socio-economic realities. In fact, one of the greatest modern Hindi poets, Gajanan Madhav Muktibodh, wrote his long poem *Andhere Mein* in the fifties — the poem is a scathing critique of the system. Interestingly, the same poet was not too critical of Nehru; in several articles he wrote sympathetically about the then prime minister.

The fronts flourished and the relations between the party and fellow-travelers strengthened. Gradually, during the fifties, Leftist ideas permeated across the entire intelligentsia. This was no mean achievement for the communists. For, not long ago, they were openly denounced for their betrayal in 1942 and ridiculed for being the lackeys of Moscow. The fronts and prominent fellow travelers helped them gain legitimacy, even respectability.

A natural corollary was the diffusion of Leftist ideals in popular culture. Hindi cinema is often castigated by Leftist critics as crude and crass, sacrificing aesthetics at the altar of commerce; and such criticism is not without substance. But it must be recognized that Hindi cinema has also been molded by people with strong Leftist leanings. Khwaja Ahmed Abbas, Balraj Sahni, Chetan Anand, Sahir Ludhianvi, Majrooh Sultanpuri, Bimal Roy, and a number of other personalities had been fellow-travelers and/or IPTA members. They may not have been the most successful people in the film industry, but their influence was undoubtedly profound.

The diffusion of could be seen at several levels in various spheres of life. In universities, Leftist ideas spread easily. This continued till the eighties, and this is something of which this writer has first-hand experience.

All major political parties have their student wings: the Congress has the National Students Union of India (NSUI); the BJP has the Akhil Bharatiya Vidyarthi Parishad (ABVP); the CPI has the All India Students Federation (AISF); and the CPM has the Students Federation of India (SFI).

The image of the NSUI has been that of an outfit of ruffians masquerading as students and enjoying the patronage of the ruling party. They were mostly fun-loving people who received loads of money from the parent party and immunity from the police — at least, till the Congress was the ruling party. These people were also helpful in organizing bandhs and rallies, collecting donations, and bullying rival candidates.

The ABVP activists were seen as antediluvian knickerwallahs, out of tune with the fast-changing world, espousing vague causes like that of cow-protection. They had nothing to offer to the youthful aspirations. They talked about a distant, glorious Golden Age which, in any case, had not any bearing on the present; or they waxed eloquent about a remote future in which the inherent "spiritual superiority" of Hinduism or India will overwhelm the "materialist" West. Not only their goals were obscure, their discourse, too, was an exercise in grandiloquent gibberish.

Only the Leftist, mainly communist, student wings had any genuine charm for students, especially bright students of the humanities stream. They could relate to the writings of Marx, Engels, Lenin, Mao, Gramski, Lukacs, EP Thompson, EH Carr, Sartre, etc. Here was the radicalism that would find a sympathetic chord among the young men and women of heightened consciousness. They found everything in Marxism — realism, idealism, a cause, romance. They got attracted to Leftist ideas, and remained wedded to them. They were the people who would dominate the intellectual class of the future. The seeds of intellectual hegemony of the Left were sown in the university campuses. Indira Gandhi would reap the windfall.

For, they provided the manpower to her who later built institutions for Leftist intellectuals to serve her purpose.

Intellectual Hegemony of the Left (2)

We saw that communist fronts started flourishing from the fifties and the relations between the party and fellow-travelers strengthened. This happened gradually but steadily. Over the years, Indian intellectuals were more and more influenced by the Left; the fronts played an important role in it, but there were also many other reasons for this.

Two things must be noted here. First, the influence of Leftists has no relation to their electoral strength. This became clear through the pressure the communists exerted on the governments of HD Deve Gowda and Inder Kumar Gujral, despite the fact that the total strength of Communists in the Lok Sabha was not even 10 per cent. Harkishan Singh Surjeet, Sitaram Yechuri, and Indrajit Gupta were among the most quoted leaders of the United Front. More than that, it was the Leftist theories about the alleged fascism and communalism of the Bharatiya Janata Party (BJP) which eventually led to its isolation and ostracism. Second, the term "Indian intellectuals" is not very clear, as there are countless social, cultural, and economic variations. Yet, we can broadly subsume this species into two categories: those who use English to convey their ideas, and those who use their mother tongues.

In an interview, French philosopher Jean-Paul Sartre said, "I don't think you can have an intellectual without his being 'Left-wing'." However, even in France this identification of intellectualism with Leftism has not been as thorough as in India, so much so that in our country the "Rightwing intellectual" seems to be a contradiction in terms. A number of factors are responsible for this unbalanced state affairs.

To begin with, many young intellectuals in the thirties and forties found socialism to be the most attractive political philosophy. They didn't have much patience for Gandhian methods, nor were they enamored of his social and economic ideas which were seen as impractical at best and retrograde at worst. Then there was the international background of the failure of capitalism, epitomized by the Depression, and the apparent success of communism, evident from the impressive results of the five-year plans in the Soviet Union. Later, the Soviet Union emerged victorious against Nazi Germany in World War II. All this left an indelible mark about the superiority of the Soviet system on many Indian youth.

Another factor was the economic condition in India; the gulf between the rich and the poor was far too wide to be ignored by people with heightened consciousness. In this context, while socialism promised a seemingly workable agenda for the country, the Rightists did not have any economic content in their philosophy. Swatantra Party stalwarts were too closely linked with princes, feudal elements, and big industry to attract any intellectual. Besides, despite all the brilliance of C Rajgopalachari and Minoo Masani, their party always gave economic reactions, never economic philosophy wedded with social reality. Similarly, the Hindutva protagonists did not have much economic content in their ideology. Their main emphasis was on the "revival of Bharatiya culture and revitalization of true Bharatiya nationalism," prohibition of cow slaughter, strengthening of Indian defence, etc. Not surprisingly, intellectuals — who had imbibed Western ideas and values of rationalism, humanism, and equality — found little merit in the agenda of the Right.

At the same time, the Establishment under Jawaharlal Nehru was committed to modernizing the country, promoting industry, and ameliorating the hardships of millions by striving towards "the socialistic pattern of society." Besides, it was liberal; whereas any number of rulers in newly-freed countries showed a predilection for dictatorship, Nehru remained a democrat. Many worshippers of Nehru have suggested at times that democracy was his gift to India. The fact, however, is that Nehru hardly ever felt the need to embrace authoritarianism — and whenever the need arose, as in 1959 when the communist government in Kerala was deposed, authoritarian measures were taken. Sardar Patel, his strongest rival, had died in 1950. Right-wing stalwarts within the Congress, like Purushottamdas Tandon, were marginalized. Many others, like JP Narayan, Acharya Narendra Deva, and Acharya Kripalani, lost their way in the deserts of Gandhian obscurities and opposition politics. Gradually, by the mid-fifties, Nehru had emerged as the pre-eminent leader of the Congress and, therefore, of the country. He was enjoying what any dictator could only dream of: unhindered power. He was the executive; the Congress-dominated legislature toed his line; his was the last word on economic affairs and foreign policy. Only the judiciary showed some reluctance, but that was not an insurmountable problem. Nehru did whatever he wanted to; among other things, he gave power to corrupt and incompetent people like VK Krishna Menon. In fact, Nehru enjoyed the best of both worlds — the unrestrained authority of a tyrant and the prestige of a liberal democrat.

His democratic credentials impressed everybody — from international personalities to Indian intellectuals. Slowly, a symbiotic relationship developed between the Establishment and intellectuals, both being of Left-liberal orientation. The flirtation which began in the Nehru era became a serious affair when Indira Gandhi took the reins of the country in her hands. The story of Raj Thapar, who authored her memoirs, *All These Years*, and her husband, Romesh, epitomizes this change. The couple, though not CPI members, were helping its leaders when the party was banned. "Underground" meetings were held at their residence. They were fed with the communist propaganda that Nehru was "a running dog of imperialism."

Romesh used to read the script of English documentaries of the Films Division. In the early fifties, he was disallowed to do this because of his political leanings. He was advised by, among others, the Urdu poet Ali Sardar Jafri to write to Nehru about the persecution he was facing. Reluctantly, Romesh "put it down on paper," wrote Raj:

> Just a couple of lines asking whether Panditji thought his voice could be subversive and if so, he had better prepare to leave India. Very simple.
>
> . . . Romesh's father's servant just delivered that letter at Panditji's residence which was just down the road for us, and we waited. The telephone bell rang at eight-thirty next morning with Nehru's secretary, MO Mathai, on the other end of the line. He introduced himself, acknowledged receipt of the letter, and said that Nehru had been agitated by it and if Romesh did not receive a call from Keskar, the Minister of Information and Broadcasting by noon, he should inform Mathai at once.
>
> We just sat back, stunned and speechless, our guilt over Nehru growing by the second as the hour of twelve approached.

The ban on Romesh was lifted. This "brush with reality left us shaky. Another bit of our myth had crumbled to nothingness. We had spent two years pouring such invective over Nehru, drowning him under a sort of cascade of words that were gradually proving to have no meaning at all, certainly no relationship to the man they adjectivised. But it was yet to take time for us to see the man for what he was, his defects we would one day assess as the very aspects we as leftists then applauded".

The Thapars were not the only intellectuals who drastically revised their views about Nehru and were attracted towards him. There were many other Left-liberal intellectuals as well who felt that the system Nehru wanted to build was essentially progressive in nature — and not without reason. Whether it was Nehru's writings, speeches, or policies — there are always undertones of modernism, secularism, and progress. In fact, Nehru could have claimed copyright over the Leftist thesis that "majority communalism" is more dangerous than "minority communalism." It won't be an exaggeration to say that he brought intellectuals close to the Establishment.

International events also helped bring the CPI close to the Congress. The Indo-Chinese war of 1962 had led to estrangement between the two nations. At the same time, the rupture between China and the Soviet Union was complete by the end of the sixties. The latter was looking for a reliable ally in the south Asian region as a bulwark against China as well as the United States; India fitted the bill. So, Indo-Soviet ties became warmer, the process culminating in the famous treaty of peace, friendship, and co-operation between India and the USSR in 1971. Concomitantly, the thesis of S Mohan Kumaramangalam was being followed in practice. Satindra Singh, who was a card-carrying member of the CPI for a decade but was disillusioned by communism, wrote in *Communists in Congress* (1973):

> Mr Kumarmangalam's "Thesis", entitled "A Review of Party Policy Since 1947", was submitted as a confidential document of the Communist Party of India (CPI) in 1964. It was then unceremoniously consigned to the Party archives. In early 1969, he submitted it again with a postscript dealing with political and economic developments in the country during the intervening period. On this occasion, the Party leadership plumped for it.

Now the conditions were ripe for the implementation of the thesis.

> Kumaramangalam's "Thesis" is to "infiltrate" the Indian National Congress, "own" its radical slogans and launch movements in support of these demands and "pressurize" the Congress leadership both within and without with the ultimate object of capturing power.

Singh adds further:

> Mr Kumaramangalam and many of his comrade-in-arms hastened to join the Congress. Some of them have now come to occupy important positions both in the government and the Congress party. Prominent among them are Mr DP Dhar, Union Minister for Planning; Mr KR Ganesh, Union Minister of State for Revenue and Expenditure; Mr Nurul Hasan, Union Minister of State for Education and Social Welfare; Mr KV Raghunath Reddy, Union Minister of State for Labor and Rehabilitation;

Mr RK Khadilkar, Union Minister of State for Health and Family Planning; Mr Chandrajit Yadav, General Secretary of the Indian National Congress; and Mr Rajni Patel, President of the Bombay Pradesh Congress Committee.

Then there were many "progressives" and fellow-travelers like Amrit Nahata, Chandra Shekhar, and Krishan Kant.

When Indira Gandhi came to power, she was seen as a dumb doll by the powerful Congress stalwarts who wielded considerable power and were the seasoned practitioners of realpolitik. That they were badly mistaken is a well-known fact today, and much has been written about it. What interests us is the methods with which she overwhelmed the formidable old guard.

The first thing she did was to lay claim over the Nehruvian legacy. Being his daughter, this proved to be quite easy. She cultivated an image of being modern, progressive, forward-looking. This made an impact on several communists, fellow-travelers, and many other intellectuals. A number of people who became her adviser were of Leftist orientation.

A Calcutta-based academic, Partha Chatterjee, wrote in the special supplement brought by *The Pioneer* on the 50th anniversary of independence:

> The [Indira Gandhi] regime was built around a political establishment. Of all Indira Gandhi's contributions this was possibly the one that has endured the longest. . . . The people she needed were not mass leaders but people with a certain technocratic competence who could be relied upon to do a job by using the machinery of government. This was the core of the new political establishment that emerged in the 1970s, mainly located for obvious reasons in the nation's Capital. It consisted of politicians who would move from one job to another at their leader's bidding, of technocrats of the public sector corporate world, of academics and professionals who ran the vast network of State agencies and semi-official institutions that advised the Government on policy matters and disbursed government grants in the fields of education, science and culture. It is a political

establishment that has survived the fall of the Indira regime, by offering its services to the successor regimes as well as by holding on to its entrenched positions within the institutions they inhabit.

Calling it "a political establishment" however, is not very appropriate: it was the Establishment, and it survived not only Indira Gandhi but also Congress rule. And it was essentially a Nehruvian Establishment, firmly committed to the cardinal principles of socialism, secularism, and non-alignment. A number of front activists and fellow-travelers became part of the Establishment. Once again, the political background provided a perfect setting for this. As a result of the Soviet Union's support for India during the Indo-Pak war of 1971, the seventies were marked by *Hindi-Russi Bhai-Bhai* sentiments. Further, the almost two-decade old affair — though there were some anxious moments in it — between the Congress and the CPI culminated in a marriage, as the two parties became formal allies. This alliance continued till 1977, but more than the politicians of the CPI, it was the fellow-travelers and Left-liberal intellectuals who enjoyed the pleasure of the honeymoon — many of them continue to enjoy the privileges to this day.

Their hegemony in the government had an ideological as well as political rationale. They became opinion-makers and, in some cases, like Jawaharlal Nehru University (JNU), which was dominated by Leftist teachers, the opinion-makers of opinion-makers. Committed Leftist activists, Left-libbers, and pinkish teenybopper intellectuals would decide the syllabi for universities, write textbooks for school students, set norms in the fields of art and culture, man the committees giving awards to creative writers, dominate edit pages of major dailies and columns of news magazines, and promote "art" cinema.

When PV Narasimha Rao and Manmohan Singh bid adieu to socialism in 1991 — and other parties, including the CPM, followed suit — a pillar of the Nehruvian edifice crumbled. Another pillar, non-alignment, had already been rendered useless in the post-Cold War era. This meant that the Left-liberal intellectuals had to religiously protect the last great pillar, secularism. Not surprisingly, it was the Leftist intellectuals who fought fiercely and relentlessly against the protagonists of Hindutva. Leftist historians, for instance, were among the foremost opponents of the BJP's claim to build the Ramjanmabhoomi Temple on the site where Babri Masjid stood. They brought out countless books, booklets, and pamphlets to prove their point; wrote innumerable articles in newspapers; and provided intellectual inputs to the Babri Masjid Action Committee. And it was the Leftist intellectuals who helped create a climate of opinion in which the BJP was seen as a communal and fascist party.

The Art of Ignoring Friends and Wooing Foes

Leftist influence on Indian foreign policy and defence matters is something which has generally gone unnoticed. Even Right-wing commentators have not properly exposed this pernicious influence.

As in most of the maladies afflicting the nation, the roots of this one, too, can be traced to the Nehru regime. Marx as well as Gandhi attracted Jawaharlal Nehru; in fact, both had cast a spell over him. Nehru was convinced of the innate goodness and grandeur of Marxism; he found merit in the theory that imperialism is the highest form of capitalism. A natural corollary was faith in beliefs that all the exploited countries in Asia, Africa, and Latin America had similar interests and could join hands for a better world, that Afro-Asian solidarity was something one could pin one's hopes on, and that socialist countries didn't launch aggression. The Leftist intellectual, VK Krishna Menon (see "Tryst with bureaucratic socialism"), played a key role in leading Nehru to the fantasyland of Thirdworldism. Even Nehru later admitted to his folly.

At the same time, it would be incorrect to say that Indian foreign policy in the fifties revolved around Leftist shibboleths; there were Gandhian ones, too — though, interestingly, both blended magically to give a synergically disastrous effect. The

Soviet-sponsored Peace Council racket — in which a number of fellow-travelers were active — accommodated Marxian as well as Gandhian influences. It must be noted that the Gandhian influence had an equally, if not more pernicious, effect on defence matters and foreign policy. Gandhians in Parliament often charged the government with wasting money on the military, which was unacceptable in the land of the Buddha, Mahavir, Nanak, and the Mahatma. Even Nehru told an army general in 1948 that the country did not need the army. It was the shock of 1962 which exorcised the ghost of Gandhi to a certain extent, but at a great cost; hundreds of Indian soldiers had to pay for it with their lives.

But the Leftist influence did not decline; if anything, it only increased over the years. An important reason for this is that, in India, foreign policy and security affairs are seldom political issues. For instance, just a few months before the general elections of 1996, lethal arms and ammunition were dropped from an aircraft at Purulia in West Bengal. The hand of Islamic fundamentalists was suspected in the mischief. But even the nationalist Bharatiya Janata Party (BJP) failed, or did not bother, to make capital out of it in the elections.

Perhaps it has something to do with mindset of Indian people; they have ignored external threats since time immemorial. From the attack of Alexander to the invasions of the Muslims, Indians have seldom taken measures to keep their frontiers guarded. The first time they showed concern was in 1962, when the outrage against the treacherous China of Mao and Chou En-lai was so great that even the ruling Congress Party — responsive as it was to the people's sentiments — demanded the head of Defence Minister Krishna Menon. Owing to his sympathy for communism and obsession for high-blown rhetoric, he was mainly responsible for the country's defeat in the India-China war. Despite being the blue-eyed boy of Nehru, Menon had to go.

As the people are not much bothered about foreign affairs, the intrusion of aristocratic Leftist intellectuals becomes easy, until, of course, somebody like Bhabani Sen Gupta — whose views are brazenly against national interests and who would like India to toe the American line — starts calling the shots in the foreign office.

How is national interest in foreign policy viewed by the Leftists? Achin Vanaik, a prominent Leftist, wrote in *The Pioneer* on 22 March 1992:

> The outspoken moralist in defence of capitalism and liberal democracy at home doubles up as the wise amoralist defending the abrogation of moral norms and democratic values in a state's external behavior, all in the name of "national interest".

Notice the contempt for "national interest." How should India respect "moral norms and democratic values" in its external behavior? By supporting, suggests Vanaik, "other causes, movements and countries be it Palestine, Iraq, Libya, [and] Latin America" and opposing "GATT and Dunkel."

There is a convergence of Leftist views and Establishment interests. All major political parties — with the exception of the BJP and its earlier avatar, the Bharatiya Jana Sangh — have generally tried their best to woo the Muslim votes. The best way to placate them, it was felt, was to blindly support the Palestine movement and the Arabs, for Indian Muslims have always shown concern for their co-religionists in other parts of the world — be it the question of Khilafat in Turkey, the Israel-Palestine conflict, or the ethnic cleansing in Bosnia. So, the Indian ruling class decided to support the Arabs against Israel, without expecting any reciprocity — in the name of lofty ideals and with an eye on the Muslim vote-bank. National interest was sacrificed at the altar of electoral politics; the Leftist justified this immorality by his sophistry and chicanery. Hence his importance. These were also the roots of the Gujral Doctrine.

Reciprocity was almost anathema to the Indian Establishment. And the country has suffered because of this. For, the Arabs and the Muslims throughout the world have always backed Pakistan against India — whether it was during the armed conflicts between the two countries, the question of Kashmir, or the meets of the Organization of Islamic Countries. Many Muslim countries have also funded and armed terrorists in Kashmir. On the other hand, Israel's friendly gestures were either ignored or scoffed at, one of them being its reported offer to bombard the nuclear plants in Pakistan.

In the late sixties, when Indira Gandhi filled her kitchen cabinet with VIP Leftists like DP Dhar, PN Haksar, and Romesh Thapar, national interest was unceremoniously dumped. A K Ray, a former secretary in the Ministry of External Affairs, wrote in *The Financial Express* (1 January 1997) about the influence of Leftist intellectuals on foreign policy during the 1971 Indo-Pak war. According to Ray, "The induction of the late DP Dhar into the affair was a tragic error. He was a complete ignoramus. It was through him that the Communist Party of India got into the act and induced a string of mistakes. Early in the second half of 1971, DP asked Maj-Gen (later Lt-Gen) JFR Jacob, Chief of Staff, Eastern Command, to arm 'communist activists' who simply did not exist because activists of the Communist Party of East Pakistan had been jailed and had been reduced to 40 members only. Jacob flatly refused, but the suggestion got known" and created apprehensions in the Awami League which was "a secularist and dedicatedly anti-communist party."

Adds Ray:

DP was obviously innocent or ignored the fact that one of the main points in Pakistani propaganda against the autonomy movement started by the Awami League was that it was an Indian conspiracy to introduce Soviet influence and "godless communism" to destroy Islam.

Further:

Early in January 1972, even before the ruling Congress of India had thought of sending a party delegation to felicitate the Awami League, and when regular travel facilities had not been fully restored, there appeared in Dhaka a large CPI delegation headed by the late Bhupesh Gupta to hail the exhumation of the Communist Party of East Pakistan and its reinstallation as the

Communist Party of Bangladesh — with less than 40 members.

Earlier, there had been the visit by Mulk Raj Anand, the much-hyped "progressive" intellectual. For his benefit, the local artists organized an exhibition of paintings reflecting the horror and anguish of the suffering people. Anand advised them to paint "not out of anger but out of love" and for "peace and harmony!" There were "imprintable reactions" of the locals. " What are these bloody Delhiwallahs after?" was the mildest comment of all. I felt thoroughly ashamed.

Ray was tracing the roots of anti-India feelings prevalent in Bangladesh, a country for whose liberation Indian soldiers shed their blood. He wrote, "There were many instances when a little practical wisdom on our part would well have earned us enormous goodwill, but somewhere in the Delhi set-up there was a terrible failure." The basic problem in the "Delhi set-up" was that, without totally extricating itself from Gandhian shibboleths (urging a people who had been recently treated barbarously to express their feelings in a pleasant manner, out of love for "peace and harmony"), it had got mired into Leftist clichés.

On the whole, Indian foreign policy has been a queer mixture of Gandhian dogmas and Leftist shibboleths. Though not many Gandhians have a say in policy-making, a number of Leftists have helped shape it.

In their scheme of things, nationalism is a snarl word and patriotism is a euphemism for jingoism. For, they believe that the poor, the "toiling masses," the subalterns, have little to do with national pride or the safety of the frontiers; they are bothered only about their bread and butter. Ergo, all sensible people should only think about improving the lot of the "toiling masses," about "moral norms and democratic values." Not surprisingly, rhetoric has prevailed over common sense and pomposity over national interest, thus rendering Indian foreign policy an abject failure.

In fact, the malaise is deeper: not only the past has been inglorious, there seems to be little hope for the future. The disdain for or ignorance of national interest is so deep-rooted that even 13-month-rule of a supposedly nationalist (jingoist to its detractors) party, the BJP, could not make any difference. Ironically, the kind of language the during the Kargil crisis was conspicuously similar to that of the Nehru government in the aftermath of the Indo-China war in 1962. Nehru talked about "betrayal"; so did Atal Behari Vajpayee.

Nehru's predicament is still understandable. His friends and foes alike called an idealist, a romantic. For decades, the Hindutva brigade lambasted him for his foreign policy blunders, and rightly so. But Nehru — an idealist, a pacifist — cannot be judged too harshly in the ultimate analysis. Saddled with the Gandhian baggage of non-violence and lacking experience, he could genuinely lament that he was betrayed. The agony of an idealist in the big, bad world of realpolitik is comprehensible.

But what about the self-proclaimed champions of realism in international affairs? The people who admire Sardar Patel and Bismarck, who quote from the *Arthshastra* and the *Mahabharata*? Nehru was misguided by Menon and fooled by Chou En-lai, but was not Vajpayee too misled by the foreign office and deceived by Nawaz Sharif?

Another, and more important, feature of the irredeemable situation is the irrational attitude towards the United States. Even after coming to power, the BJP did not do anything to change the old, socialist anti-Americanism that infests the foreign office. Indian reaction to the US bombing on the Sudan and Afghanistan was the height of stupidity. The BJP-led government *opposed* the American campaign against Osama bin Laden. This despite the fact that the BJP is committed to oppose Islamic fundamentalism, and bin Laden is the fount of terrorism and fundamentalism in several parts of the world and his role is also suspected in Kashmir.

Nothing could be more ludicrous or absurd as this criticism, a result of deep-rooted, pathological anti-Americanism. A typical Leftist syndrome.

Summary

It seems surprising that communists, who were seen as Quislings because of their treacherous role during the Quit India Movement of 1942, and their sympathizers and like-minded people gained so much prominence in such a short time. One reason was, of course, the intellectual bankruptcy of the Right, or whatever passes in its name. In any case, there is no denying the fact that the Left was able to establish its intellectual hegemony in various spheres of life. So much so that even the most absurd assertions of progressive intellectuals and the most opportunistic moves of Leftist politicians often go unscathed. Whether it is the writing of history, domination in academics and academia, or determining the foreign policy principles and parameters, the Left has left it indelible mark on everything. That too, without the required electoral mandate.

CHAPTER 2

Techniques of Hegemony

Left-wing Apriorism

The capacity of Leftists to make empirically unverified and unverifiable assertions is remarkable. Even more remarkable is the fact that these assertions often enjoy the status of self-evident truths.

Some of the Leftist dogmas have absolutely nothing to do with experience or common sense. One of them is that the Bharatiya Janata Party (BJP) is an upper caste, upper class, north Indian party and, therefore, can't represent the masses of the country. This is a very comforting dogma: the rise of the BJP is explained in terms of its "rabble-rousing" tactics; but, in the end, all will be well, as it happens in Hindi movies. People will see reason and dump this reactionary party. Only if wishes were horses!

What the Leftists refuse to recognize is the fact that the BJP graph is as steady as it has been steep. From two seats in 1984 to the 13-day government of Atal Behari Vajpayee in 1996 and then again in 1998, the party has gained in terms of seats, voting percentage, social penetration, geographical reach, and political acceptability. True that at one time, indeed till as late as the early eighties, it was mainly supported by upper castes in the Hindi belt only. But in the late eighties and early nineties, its base expanded socially as well as geographically. In fact, it grew only as a result of its sustained efforts to attract non-upper caste people. And one need not be a psephologist to see this; but one has to discard the Leftist dogmas and apriorism.

In the eighteenth century Western philosophy, a term widely used was *a priori*, which means independent of experience or empirical evidence. Wherever there is smoke, there is fire; the sun rises in the east; every physical object is attracted towards the earth by the gravitational force — these are all experienced by us. But there is no reason to believe, it was argued, that these truths will hold at all times: that is, there is no certainty that some day smoke could be without fire; that the sun won't rise in the west; that physical objects won't fly away. But, claimed the eighteenth century philosophers, nobody in his right senses could say some day two times two would be anything but four. The truths of mathematics are *a priori*: they are independent of experience, as the truth "two plus two is four" is independent of any empirical evidence.

Indian Leftists do not hold the metaphysical apriorism of Western philosophy in high esteem, but they do subscribe to so many apriorisms in political, social, economic, cultural, and economic matters. The most important characteristic of Leftwing apriorism is a neat categorization, between good and evil, secular and communal, progressive and reactionary. The BJP is communal and, therefore, bad, regressive, fascist, reactionary, evil, etc. When the Samajwadi Party (SP) and the Bahujan Samaj Party (BSP) in Uttar Pradesh in 1993 joined hands to form the government against the BJP, it was seen as a dream come true. Here was a party representing backward castes and Muslims (SP) and another representing Dalits (BSP); it was a veritable rainbow coalition — all the dispossessed, under-privileged groups uniting to combat an allegedly pro-upper class, pro-upper caste, anti-poor party.

It was a case of unadulterated apriorism, and the categorization, influenced by the Mandal wave, was total: the BJP represented *all* the upper caste and affluent people; the SP represented *all* the backward people and Muslims; the BSP, *all* the Dalits. Further, *all* the upper castes were privileged; *all* the backwards, Muslims, and Dalits were among the exploited, oppressed, and repressed. Many Leftist intellectuals saw the seeds of a bigger, national-level rainbow coalition in the SP-BSP alliance. Such a coalition followed naturally from the alliance — in the manner as proofs are reached in the theorems of geometry and conclusions arrived at in deductive logic.

Unfortunately for the Leftists, politics is more than logic. As it turned out, the so-called rainbow coalition was no more than a marriage of convenience which ended in a bitter divorce. Later, the BSP, supposedly the radical party of the wretched of the earth, twice allied with the allegedly statusquoist BJP.

Another instance of apriorism is the Leftists' attitude towards popular TV serials of the eighties, *Ramayana* and *Mahabharata*. There is no empirical evidence indicating that these serials affected the voting pattern in favor of the BJP; no survey was ever conducted; no opinion poll organized. Only a few Left-liberal intellectuals found the contemporaneity of the two serials and the BJP's rise to be conspicuous; and this conspicuousness was seen as causation. Some more imaginative writers saw a conspiracy to saffronize culture. Ramanand Sagar (who made *Ramayana*), BR Chopra (who made *Mahabharata*), and top bureaucrats in the Information and Broadcasting Ministry were accused of working on a hidden agenda (Interestingly, these were also the bureaucrats who arranged the telecast of the anti-Hindu and the anti-Sikh film, *Tamas*, on television under Rajiv Gandhi's rule).

The fact is that the Ramanand Sagars and the BR Chopras make any serial or movie for money. Sagar produced *Alif Laila* whose production quality was as bad as that of *Ramayana*. But the point is that this serial highlighted the glories of Islam. Similarly, Sanjay Khan had no compunctions in making *Jai Hanuman*, a serial in which "Jai Shri Ram," the war cry of the votaries of Hindutva, is heard frequently. But this does not make Khan a closet knickerwallah. (But had Khan not been a Muslim, he might have been accused of promoting communalism). He and people of his ilk are professionals, businessmen, not cultural commissars or die-hard ideologues.

The allegations against Doordarshan officials — that they encouraged "communal serials" — were even more ludicrous; in fact, calling them Hindutva sympathizers is a kind of honor, for they were interested in making money rather than promoting cultural nationalism of the BJP variety. Had any of the Leftist writers met any of the serial makers, he or she would have known the otherwise well-known fact that in the clearance of Doordarshan serials what matters is the amount of bribe, not ideological tilt. But for this, the Leftist writer has to shed *a priori* doctrines and face empirical evidence squarely. This seems to be a tall order.

The Masses Are Not the Masses

What are the masses? The Indian communists never tried to understand them in their entirety, i.e., in the proper social, economic, cultural, political, and religious setting. Here, too, they relied on apriorism. They sought to be fitted into the straitjacket of an imported ideology. The best, or worst, example of this straitjacketing can be seen in a movie, *Naya Sansar*, made by the well-known fellow-traveler, Khwaja Ahmed Abbas. The cast included Sheikh Mukhtar, Sitara Devi, the well-known dancer, and Akhtari Bai, who later became famous as ghazal singer Begum Akhtar.

The protagonist, Sheikh Mukhtar, is not only a man but also the (Marxist) history of man. He is shown living in a primitive commune, totally unaware of private property and the evil consequences associated with it like acquisitiveness, selfishness, greed, and rapacity. He is the noble savage-cum-Luddite rebel-cum-secular champion-cum-progressive hero; he is the embodied *volk geist* of what communists consider as the masses. This is not to suggest that all Leftist film makers, writers, and artists have as simplistic and shallow worldview as Abbas had; some of them have indeed explored the complexity and intricacies of India in their works; but when it comes to theorization, a worldview similar to that of Abbas holds sway. The masses are seen as a homogeneous chunk bereft of caste bias, class prejudice, feudal hangover, cultural differences, and religious strife. Such unpleasant facts are explained in economic terms; they are, Marxist thinkers argue, the result of "false consciousness".

Earlier, the communists seldom took the institution of caste into account while theorizing about the masses, society, or politics. Not that it was never mentioned, but it was shown as a product and function of class struggle. A natural corollary was the neglect of peasants, as many major communist theoreticians had a low opinion about rural masses.

In the early years of Independence, there was of course the debate whether India should adopt the Russian path to revolution (with the proletariat as the bulwark) or the Chinese path (with peasantry as the main support). But, as usual, the debate was inspired by Mao's success rather than by the existing conditions in India. Little, if any, effort was made to know the preparedness or even the willingness of peasantry to go for a communist revolution.

But in the wake of Independence, as at other times, the communists assumed that they represented the people, that the people were ready to storm "the Congress Bastilles". We know that Don Quixote mistook windmills for demons, but it is not clear what the communists mistook for "the Congress Bastilles"! There were two reasons for the communists' belief in the willingness of the people for revolution. One was that their bosses in Moscow were not favorably disposed towards Nehru at the time of Independence. The second was the communists' perception of the people, the masses; they were seen not *as they were* but *as they ought to be* — progressive, forward-looking, bereft of any bias, prejudice, parochialism, and fanaticism; in short, the people were the People and the masses, the Masses. And who else could lead them better than the communists who know all about Marx, Engels, and Lenin? The Second Congress of the CPI held in Calcutta in February 1947 adopted a radical line. It maintained that "though the bourgeois leadership parade the story that independence has been won, the fact is that the freedom movement has been betrayed and the national leadership has struck a treacherous deal behind the back of the starving people, betraying every slogan of the democratic revolution." The comrades knew everything about the "deal" and the "starving people", thanks to their great clairvoyance.

Sir Richard Tottenham, additional secretary, Home, who played a key role in persuading communists to become Quislings during the Quit India Movement, wrote on 23 March 1943, "The communists are the sort of people who must always be 'anti' something rather than 'pro' anything (except, perhaps, themselves and a shadow entity called 'people')." Sometimes, imperial officials are more observant and sharp-witted than the finest savants. For, the "people" indeed remain a "shadow entity" in Marxian discourse. When the (real) people metamorphose into People, they become imperceptible to ordinary perception; then you need clairvoyance — known as dialectics in Marxist parlance — to perceive them.

Edmund Burke wrote in a letter to an acquaintance in 1790:

I have no great opinion of that sublime abstract, metaphysic reversionary, contingent humanity, which in *cold blood* can subject the *present time* and those we *daily see and converse with* to immediate calamities in favor of the *future and uncertain* benefit of the persons who *only exist in idea* (emphases in the original).

Most of the time, Indian communists have championed the cause of the People who are a "shadow entity" and a "sublime abstract," much different from the people "we daily see and converse with." Since they are an abstraction, a transcendental, *a priori* concept, anything could be said about them. It is like talking about the *brahman* of Vedanta, God of Semitic theology, or the Absolute Spirit of Hegelian idealism. As the People had nothing to do with verifiable experience or data, they could be assumed to be in any state of mind.

Not that the presentation of abstract Masses has never been noticed by any Leftist. Rustom Bharucha wrote *In the Name of the Secular* (Oxford University Press, 1998) on contemporary cultural activism, citizenship, and nationalism. According to him:

> The possibility of a revolutionary consciousness emerging from within the "folk", however "infantile", is simply not addressed. The model of liberation is simply determined. This, in essence, is the continued problematic of a secularist critique of traditional arts, which refuses to acknowledge the liberatory possibilities of religion, or more specifically, of religious material transformed into another kind of cultural discourse through oral narrative or performance, which functions with its own norms, quirks, grammar, levels of interruption, and inscriptions of the worldly and the political. At one level, the prejudice against religious narratives (or what passes as "religious") is concretized through the imposition of secularist categories. At another, it reveals the tremendous distance of the advocates of "people's art" from the actual contexts in which people create and interpret an art for themselves.

It is worth noting out here that when the activists of the IPTA represented "the people" in totally secular, realist narratives, without the mediation of traditional and folk resources, these representations were not always understood by the people themselves. The landmark production of *Nabanna* (1944) on the Bengal famine, for instance, which revolutionized the representation of the subaltern on the Indian stage, did not always succeed in eliciting an immediate response from audiences in district towns, who were not familiar with the dramaturgical and technological innovations of the play. A particularly revealing observation has been made by the primary activist of the IPTA movement, Sudhi Pradhan, who recalled how during a performance of a one-act play on famine, *Jalabandi*, in the 24-Parganas district, a peasant leader (Khoka Roy) had "rushed backstage to persuade the performers to supply a commentary since the peasants could not understand anything." It is through such illustrations of actual theater practice that one begins to respect the tremendous challenge that the IPTA activists faced in establishing communication with audiences in non-urban locations.

In this context, the popular television soap opera *Nukkad*, too, needs to be discussed. Its protagonists are the true representatives of the Masses. They are the have-nots of the society, supposedly inhabiting every nook and corner of the country, as the title of the serial itself suggests. (It is another matter that such nooks and corners, *nukkads*, exist only in the minds of Leftist artists). The only thing the protagonists can boast of is their humanity, the concern they have for each other. Their hearts brim with love and affection. They have different backgrounds; some of them are Muslims; but, on the whole, they are the Masses. And they know that they are the Masses. Whenever they talk about each other, they often put *apna* (our) before the name — *apna* Khopdi, *apna* Guru, etc. They are simple people, whose sole concerns are bread and butter. They don't have any caste biases, regional prejudices, or communal feelings. When there is a communal riot, they don't get swayed by fanaticism. For, they are not under the spell of "false consciousness"; they are blessed with "true consciousness"; they are progressive.

The communists have been obsessed with the abstractions and apriorism of ideology. One such *a priori* concept is that all the exploited people are essentially progressive. Many Bengali communists were, however, shocked when they discovered that the poor rickshawpuller of Calcutta — whose pathos and plight was immortalized by Balraj Sahni in Bimal Roy's *Do Bigha Zamin* — becomes a ruthless martinet when he goes back to his native village in Bihar and buys some land there. He exploits agricultural laborers in a manner that would put any Hindi film zamindar to shame. Between pitiable plight to formidable might, there is only one step.

While communists ignored the reality of caste, the socialists, particularly those of the Lohiaite-Mandalite brand, went to the other extreme: they laid conspicuously excessive emphasis on caste. Lohia went on proclaiming that in India class war assumes the form of caste war. So, whereas the communists tried to explain everything in economic terms, the socialists tried to do the same in social, or caste, terms. And when Vishwanath Pratap Singh bestowed respectability on caste politics, even communists started seeing some substance in socialistic assertions.

Singh took caste-based ideology to its extreme. Not only that, he also supported his ideology with electoral arithmetic: since upper caste Hindus, who are also the upper class haves in the Mandalite theology, constitute only 10 per cent of the total population, it is possible to unite the rest of the 90 per cent under the banner of Mandal or social justice and secularism. But, unfortunately for Singh, politics is more than arithmetic and Indian society is more than the caste system. In theory, mobilization on Mandalite lines seemed plausible to certain ideologues and politicians; in practice, it has proved to be a quixotic adventure.

For, the theory is based on too neat a schematization — 10 per cent haves and 90 per cent have-nots. One need not be a sociologist to know that every upper caste person is not privileged or "elitist", nor is every backward person poor. Further, there are as many, if not more, contradictions and conflicts between the backwards and dalits as between upper castes and lower castes. In the villages of UP and Bihar, the Yadavs and Kurmis are often as merciless oppressors of the dalits as are the Rajputs and Bhumihars. The bitterness between the Samajwadi Party of Mulayam Singh Yadav and the Bahujan Samaj Party of Mayavati is not only because of personal reasons; it is sustained by the subterranean socio-economic factors, the most important of which being the backward castes' disdain for dalits and the antagonistic land relations.

The English-speaking Leftists in metropolitan cities — who set the intellectual agenda and who are more exposed to Western discourses than they are aware of the ground realities — were ecstatic when Yadav and Mayavati allied in 1993 to stop Kalyan Singh from coming to power in UP. The grand vision of VP Singh seemed to be unfolding. The backwards and dalits, presumably the subalterns and have-nots, had joined hands to check the onslaught of fascist, anti-poor forces. A prominent Leftist intellectual actually wrote on the edit page of *The Times of India* that the magic mantra to contain communal forces had been formulated and it was the unity of all marginalized groups (including minorities) against majoritarianism. The containment of the BJP was inevitable. Or so it appeared.

For, the supposedly marginalized groups were hardly a homogeneous entity; there were, and are, too many fissures to be cemented by rhetoric. In the first place, the backward people, whose interests Mulayam Singh Yadav claimed to represent, are often dominant castes like the Yadavs and Gujjars; and only the uninformed would call the dominant castes as "marginalized". They often treat dalits like cattle. Besides caste biases, there are also economic reasons: dalits often work as laborers on the lands of dominant castes, which frequently leads to arguments and worse.

Then there are the Muslims. They may be voting for the parties championing the cause of social justice, but this does not make them an egalitarian community.

In other words, the masses are not what Westernized Leftists and Lohiaite-Ambedakarite socialists think they are; their thinking is based on apriorism and has little to do with facts. The masses are not the Masses.

Yet, this identification helps make fantastic assertions and comical claims. So, MN Roy could write in 1924 without looking like a fool, "The masses are very restive. The peasantry is a veritable inflammable material, while the city proletariat demonstrates its revolutionary zeal whenever there is an opportunity. The process of uniting all revolutionary elements into an anti-imperialist army is going on steadily. . . . The people will see that the reformist programme of the bourgeoisie does not lead anywhere. . . ." Roy could see everything about the Masses — "inflammable" peasantry, the "revolutionary zeal" of the proletariat — while racketeering in Russia and other Western countries; he did not need any factual support to substantiate his assertions which were the product of the abstractions he was toying with. Similarly, Rajani Palme-Dutt could thunder in 1926, "Only a new national movement based on the workers' and peasants, and with a political and social programme expressing the interests of the masses, can bring new life. The conditions for this are ripe." Sitting in England, he knew that the conditions were ripe for a new movement and the Congress leadership had ceased to be progressive. He could have written all this sitting on the moon, for he knew the Truth, i.e., Marxism. According to the 1951 program of the CPI, "It is also a deception of the people to say that under the new constitution the masses or the government elected by them can work their way to freedom and happiness." Even today, Harkishan Singh Surjeet and Sitaram Yechuryof the CPM and AB Bardhan of the CPI can sell any absurd idea in the name of combating communalism, checking the fascist forces from occupying the center-stage, and promoting a pro-People political formation.

Secular McCarthyism

Vishwanath Pratap Singh, in an interview given to the news magazine, *Outlook* (1 September 1997), said, "In our political debate, the importance of the political space is usually missed out. Therefore, when we speak of secular political forces, the focus is on their occupying the ruling political space. However, the threat to secularism is not over till the opposition space is also to a large extent shared by another secular force." In other words, another call for a pro-People formation.

On the face of it, the ideal situation Singh dreamt of seemed too bizarre to be true. The United Front government was in power when Singh spoke to the *Outlook* correspondent. The various constituents of the UF were bound by their fear of and hatred for the Bharatiya Janata Party (BJP), the so-called communal force. Singh, who was sort of guru to the ruling front, was not satisfied with this: he wanted the secularists to be in power as well as in opposition!

Or so it appeared.

For, what Singh was suggesting was something sinister rather than bizarre; he wanted to banish the biggest political party; he wanted the voice of crores of people, who had reposed their faith in the BJP, to be throttled: the Mandal messiah was alluding to a form of McCarthyism. In VP Singh's scheme of things, Hindu nationalism doesn't deserve to exist; it has to be marginalized, suppressed, and, if possible, annihilated. ·

At the same time, it must be noted that Singh was not saying anything very controversial; the political alchemy he wanted to perfect to defeat the BJP might have proved a non-starter at that time — as it was debunked by all major UF constituents — but Singh was not accused of being politically immoral, fascistic, or anti-democratic (if the attempt to silence the voice of millions of people is not fascist and anti-democratic, nothing else is). The climate of opinion at that time was such that Singh's alchemy was ridiculed but not denounced. How was this climate of opinion built?

Girilal Jain, in his book *The Hindu Phenomenon* (1994), has talked about "the liberal-Marxist-Gandhian idiom." It is "the idiom in which the public discourse has been conducted in our country for over seven decades, that is, since the ascendancy of the Gandhi-Nehru leadership in the freedom movement." As the name suggests, the idiom is a mixture of liberalism, Marxism, and Gandhism — each of the ingredients getting "emasculated" in the process of merger. Jain has discussed how what was rotten in the Indian tradition became part of this idiom; "the crippling 'ideals' of poverty, austerity, indifference to social reality and power came to be widely cherished" down the ages; these 'ideals' were glorified by the liberal-Marxist-Gandhian elite. Jain adds that "the bhakti psychology was. . . powerfully reinforced (in the Muslim period). This psychology explains the easy acceptance by the urban Hindu elite (in the modern age) of the alien concepts of liberalism and Marxism."

Though Jain recognized the significance of the liberal-Marxist-Gandhian idiom, he did not study its genesis. The idiom started taking shape in the twenties when Mahatma Gandhi took over the reins of the national movement. An important feature of the theory and practice of Gandhian ideology is its inclusiveness. Gandhi wanted all Indians — rich and poor, landlords and peasants, industrialists and workers, capitalists and socialists, Hindus and Muslims, upper castes and harijans — to unite in the fight against British imperialism. He got so obsessed with the idea of inclusiveness that he bent backwards to accommodate the demands of the groups which were not keen on joining the mainstream. At times, he was even seen to be compromising the interests of the sections that were already in the mainstream. This was the beginning of appeasement.

The votaries of Hindutva have often accused the Congress and other leaders of appeasing the Muslims; the alliance with the Khilafatists is cited as an example. Lurking behind the Khilafat movement was the Moplah rebellion in Kerala in the early twenties. According to Khalid Bin Sayeed in *Pakistan: The Formative Phase, 1858–1947* (Oxford University Press), in the rebellion, "Hindu houses were sacked, temples desecrated, and thousands of Hindus converted. . . . The Moplahs were not only rising against Hindu zamindars but were also converting by force Hindus who did not help them. . . . In the Central Legislature it was decided that, according to the Madras Government, the number of conversions by force ran into thousands. But the Congress Working Committee did not want to hurt the Muslim feelings by denouncing in too strong terms the Moplah outrages against Hindu religion, life and property."

Gandhi was determined to placate any leader who claimed to be championing the cause of any community. (Interestingly, Gandhi's alliance with the Khilafatists was against his own principle that there should be harmony between means and ends. For, Gandhi's end was to bring the Muslims to the mainstream. They supported him because they wanted the Khilafat in Turkey to be restored, not because they wanted India to be freed. Gandhi knew that, yet he sought their support. It didn't matter to Gandhi what the ultimate objectives of the Muslims were as long as they supported him against the British. Ends justified means.)

The Ali brothers, who were in the forefront of the Khilafat movement, at least had a mass following. But Gandhi also tried to appease a self-styled and self-serving leader of the harijans like BR Ambedkar who was an unabashed collaborator of the colonial rulers. He hardly had any following — in any case, it was negligible when compared to that of Gandhi. But Gandhi made the famous Poona Pact with him in 1932. In other words, Gandhian inclusiveness was not natural but contrived and tokenist.

Not surprisingly, the nationalist sentiment was deprived of the religious fervor — motherland, *vande mataram, et al.* — and patriotic ardor, so poignant in the thoughts of Bankim Chandra Chatterjee, Tilak, Lala Lajpat Rai, Bipin Chandra Pal, and Aurobindo Ghosh. The kernel of Indian nationalism slowly but steadily shriveled.

Meanwhile Leftist influence added a new dimension to nationalism. The economic content of the nationalist movement became more important. Whereas Marxian ideas had rejuvenated nationalism in countries like Russia, China, Cuba, and Vietnam, they stifled its growth in India, as we shall see in another chapter. By the thirties, a number of intellectuals were convinced that political independence without economic content and social emancipation was meaningless. It would tantamount to "replacing John with Govind", said the famous Hindi writer Premchand. And Leftist ideas were seeping in literature, art, culture, and generally in public discourse.

In such a milieu, Jawaharlal Nehru created an image of himself which helped him grow in stature — the image of a young socialist who wanted total restructuring of the economy and the society, an internationalist (he participated in the pro-communist anti-fascist league in Brussels in 1927), a liberal, and an intellectual. Besides, he was thoroughly Westernized, and this trait made him popular among the numerically insignificant but immensely influential intelligentsia. Before independence, he did not have much mass following. In 1928, when he became Congress president for the first time, Pandit Madan Mohan Malviya opposed him by saying that his only qualification was that he was the son of Motilal Nehru But Jawaharlal Nehru overcame the drawback of lack of following by becoming close to Mahatma Gandhi. The views of the two men on a variety of important issues were divergent. Gandhi could read the pulse of the people; Nehru could not do that, but he did read the pulse of Gandhi; and this served the purpose: he became independent India's first prime minister.

Despite their disagreements, the basic structures of their ideologies were not much dissimilar. Inclusivism was as much a cardinal principle of Gandhi as it was of Nehru. So, Nehru invited Ambedkar to join the Union cabinet — an exercise in tokenism to show the State's resolve to involve the downtrodden at the highest level. To the Left-liberal predilections of Nehru were added the worst features of Gandhian philosophy like mindless pacifism. Hence the country got an Establishment which was trying to cope with the conflicting pulls of liberalism, Marxism, and Gandhism. And since ruling ideas are the ideas of ruling classes, public discourse has always been conducted in our country in the liberal-Marxist-Gandhian idiom.

This idiom has played a key role in the creation of a climate of opinion in which Leftist and Left-liberal theories have thrived.

Defending the Indefensible

One question has always intrigued this writer: why is it that anything that is almost always repugnant to common sense enjoys the Left's sympathy, if not downright support? Take the case of Rabri Devi, whose coronation as Bihar's chief minister was widely seen as an utterly cynical and brazen move by Laloo Prasad Yadav. The man in the street was aghast by such a mockery of democracy, decency, and propriety. But not Leftist intellectuals and think-tanks. Ashok Mitra, former minister in the Jyoti Basu government, was one of them.

In an article in *The Pioneer* on 6 August 1997, Mitra lampooned "the prim people" who "think they have the exclusive right of defining and defending democratic norms in this country. . . . There indignation spills over at the spectacle of Ms Rabri Devi. . . . The buffoon of a husband is precluded from holding office, the wife is summoned from the kitchen to be his formal stand-by. This is the pits; declare editorial writers. . .; this is the pits, echo constitutional and political science pundits." Further, "by holding Ms Rabri Devi to ridicule, the snooty ones are only betraying their class bias. To draw a parallel between the classy dynasty still presiding over New Delhi and [what] a few rustlers have set up in Patna is apparently not a legitimate exercise. When people of the noble order found a dynasty, their credentials are not questioned. It is a different matter if the bug of dynastic aspiration bites the rustic crowd who have risen from the ranks of one of the Mandal or Dalit communities."

The subtext of Mitra's article has dangerous overtones: since the Nehru-Gandhi family has been tolerated, there is nothing wrong in accepting Rabri Devi; so much indignation against her accession was because she, "the daughter of one goatherd and married to another, belongs to the lower depths not normally mentioned in the salons of the bold and the beautiful"; this indignation "is a variant of class war."

So, Mitra provided Laloo with the veneer of ideology. But he was not alone in doing so; there were any number of other Leftists as well who were indirectly helping Laloo — but they were slightly different from the old-fashioned Comrade Mitra. Their phraseology was couched in the language of political correctness, the fashion of the day; they talked about caste prejudice, gender bias, "upper caste elite", etc. According to Brinda Karat of the All India Democratic Women's Association, a CPM outfit, "I think this outrage is extremely hypocritical — it's shameful the way educated people are flinching at Rabri Devi's kitchen-to-CM transition." Similarly, Indu Agnihotri of the Janawadi Mahila Samity said, "The bias is against the Rabris of the world — not against the Sonias and the Priyankas." Praful Bidwai, a Leftist columnist, wrote in *The Frontline* (5 September 1997): "At work here often is the elite's arrogant, casteist prejudice against people of humbler social origin, lacking 'education' and the 'sophistication' of the urban elite." Not to be left behind, film-maker Anand Patwardhan told a newspaper that the Rabri affair was less dangerous "than the things we tolerate in this country such as the fascist government in Maharashtra."

Further, added Patwardhan, "nobody minds Harshad Mehta and Narasimha Rao but Laloo is intolerable because of the way he looks and speaks."

The entire defence of Laloo and Rabri was based on the premise that never before was any voice raised against the dynastic aspirations of the Nehru-Gandhi family and no upper caste leader ever had been condemned because of corruption. Needless to say, the premise has nothing to do with reality. Any number of leaders, parties, writers, and commentators — their ideological leanings ranging from the Left to the Right — have berated the dynastic rule of the Nehru-Gandhis. Similarly, numerous upper caste ministers and chief ministers have been accused of corrupt practices, and many have actually paid dearly because of these accusations. Rajiv Gandhi, who had all the "sophistication of the urban elite", lost prime-ministership because of the kickback charges only. So, it makes no sense in saying that "nobody minds Harshad Mehta and Narasimha Rao", that upper caste upper class politicians are not affected by the allegations of venality, that "Laloo is intolerable because of the way he looks or speaks." True, Laloo's appearance, utterances, mannerism, and antics evoke sarcastic comments, but similar is the reaction to the buffoonery of upper caste leaders like Kalpanath Rai, too.

Leftist intellectuals can say that they were not defending — directly or indirectly — Laloo and Rabri; they were just attacking the upper caste, upper class bias in the criticism of the drama staged in Patna. But the fact is that the Leftist argument had no moral or rational basis; it was guided by political calculation. Laloo was seen, despite all his faults, as the last barrier to check the saffron wave in Bihar. True, he is corrupt, uncouth, brash, but he is secular; he fights against "communal forces." Therefore, he has to be shielded. An all-out Leftist attack on Laloo could mean weakening the communist-socialist alliance. Hence the defence, though in an oblique manner. Since you can't directly defend your rogue ally, use a perverse logic: true, he is bad, but others are also bad; ergo, in the big bad world, his badness is not to be condemned.

Hindu — A Snarl Word

If a potential ally has to be defended by all means, fair and foul, the potential enemy too has to be maligned, by hook or by crook. Hence the denigration of the Hindu community.

To a large section of the intellectual class, the word "Hindu" stands for all that is rotten, obscurantist, retrograde, slothful, iniquitous, and inhuman in India. Hindus are the most backward-looking, hypocritical, cowardly people: their society is caste-ridden and oppressive; their economy can't grow beyond a point; their past is full of ignominious defeats; and their future is bleak.

Or many leading intellectuals believe so.

However, it was not like that all the time. Till the second decade of the twentieth century, it was the Hindu idiom in which all nationalist discourse was conducted. Hindu nationalism and Indian nationalism were indistinguishable. As nationalism was deHinduized, first under Mahatma Gandhi and then under Jawaharlal Nehru, and as the liberal-Marxist-Gandhian idiom found recognition, the denigration of Hinduism started. It was Nehru who set the ball rolling by enunciating the theory that "majority communalism" is more dangerous than "minority communalism." For, though the latter may cause a few law-and-order problems and be a nuisance in politics, it is the former which can play havoc with the entire country. Therefore, goes the line of argument, majority communalism is nothing but fascism, nazism, etc; the consequences would be far-reaching; if the Hindus come under its spell, they will try to annihilate the Muslims as the Germans tried to exterminate the Jews under Hitler. There would be saffron Auschwitz and Dachau. So, Hindu communalism has to be fought "at any cost". Mulayam Singh Yadav and Harkishen Singh Surjeet have often used these words.

Denigrating Hinduism has been an old strategy of Leftists in their battle against Hindutva. They have played a key role in making "Hindu" a snarl word. Being the most consistent Macaulayans, they only saw the gloomy, seamier side of India and Hinduism. The denigrate-Hinduism project was a total operation; it made its presence felt not only in the political arena but also in the fields of academics and academia, media, art, and culture. It was suggested that India can never achieve an economic growth rate of more than 3.5 per cent. Hindus, as everybody knows, are slothful, fatalistic, superstitious, ritualistic, and pusillanimous people; they lack enterprise. Hence "the Hindu rate of growth."

In historiography, Leftist scholars have tried to underestimate the contributions of Hindus and magnify their shortcomings. Communist historian DN Jha thundered that there was never a "golden age" in ancient India; it was no more than a myth. Another Marxist historian, RS Sharma, propounded the theory that the Gupta period, which had been identified with the Golden Age by nationalist historians, actually contained the seeds of decay and debilitating feudalism. Anything that belongs to ancient or Hindu India is bad, retrograde, and reactionary. Raj Thapar mentions an interesting anecdote in her memoirs, *All These Years*, "Sitting with Mohan (Kumaramangalam, an important communist leader) once, having a cup of tea, he asked me what I had named my daughter. When I said 'Malavika,' he rolled those marble black eyes of his and said, 'You better be careful, Raj, that's a reactionary name and like this you might slowly find yourself on the other side of the fence.' I was aghast and controverted with him, passionately explaining how I had kept this name locked securely in my consciousness ever since I read Kalidas' *Malavika Agnimitra* in college." It's not just the *Manusmriti* but all ancient Hindu classics, and anything Hindus can be proud of, that are "reactionary". ·

Anti-Hindu bias becomes apparent when Leftist historians discuss the Muslim conquest of India. Khaliq Ahmad Nizami in *A Comprehensive History of India* (People's Publishing House, a pro-communist set-up which was flourishing during the Indo-Soviet *bhai-bhai* days) has blamed Hindu society for the Muslim conquest. The Rajput polity was weakened by incessant bickerings. But this political system, continues Nizami, "reflected the basic weakness of the social structure of the time.

The principle of caste, which formed the basis of the Indian social system in the 11th and 12th centuries, had annihilated all sense of common citizenship and killed all patriotic sentiments. . . ." Further, "the invidious caste distinctions. . . rendered the whole military organization rickety and weak."

Such has been the sway of the liberal-Marxist-Gandhian idiom and the deep-rootedness of anti-Hindu bias that nobody bothered to point out that the twelfth century social conditions can't be judged by the twentieth century morals. Yet, most of the normative statements about the Indian social structure are made assuming that the authors of the *dharmashastras* of that period had read Voltaire and Rousseau, Bacon and Mill, Marx and Engels — and yet they willfully ignored the views of such great people. Nobody cared to challenge the oppressive-Hindu-society-egalitarian-Islam theory. However, the fact is that the Muslim community in India, right from the beginning, has been as hierarchical and iniquitous as Hindu society. There has been a clear-cut division between the Ashraf (the respectable and the respected, the Muslim counterpart of *bhadralok*; they claim their superior status because of their foreign descent) and the Ajlaf (the plebeians). Zarina Bhatty blasted the egalitarian Islam theory in her essay 'Social Stratification among Muslims in India' in *Caste: Its Twentieth Century Avatar* (edited by MN Srinvas and published by Viking Penguin India). She studied Muslim society at Kasauli (a pseudonym), a Muslim village in Uttar Pradesh. She writes: "Muslim status groups and their structuring in Kasuali come close to the Hindu caste system. Although notions of purity and impurity have no scriptural sanction in Islam, occupations are hierarchically arranged on the basis of these ideas, the degrees of impurity of the occupation being a major determinant of the rank of a caste." Further, "interactions between the *oonchi zat* (high caste) and the *neechi zat* (low caste) are regulated by established patron-client relationships of the jajmani system. . . . Like the Ashraf castes, which are arranged hierarchically, the non-Ashraf castes also relate to each other in a hierarchical manner."

Then there are unclean castes which are associated with polluting or unclean professions, like handling human excreta. "Among the Muslims, if a person accidentally touches an individual of an unclean caste, the former must purify himself with a simple bath, particularly prior to performing a religious function like saying 'namaz,' reading the Koran or entering a mosque. There is a difference between the Muslims and Hindus, and it lies in the fact that, unlike among Hindus, no elaborate rituals are prescribed for Muslims for purifying themselves in the event of physical contact with an individual from an unclean caste."

In other words, Muslim society is as much, if not more, hierarchically stratified and oppressive as Hindu society. The high and low castes, the patron-client system, the purity-pollution complex, untouchability — the Muslims have them all. Yet, it was only Hindu society which has been accused for being rigid, caste-ridden, and oppressive. Writes Bhatty, "It is unfortunate that for long the Muslims of the subcontinent failed to attract the attention of anthropologists who studied this region." It was not unfortunate or a result of the fortuitous circumstances; studying Muslim society could have been a good academic exercise, but could never have attained as much success as studying and denigrating Hindu society.

It was because of the sustained denigrate-Hinduism project that the Mandalite ideology found legitimacy and wide acceptance. The Mandal Commission report is full of anecdotes, quotes, and references telling how unjust, rigid, and iniquitous Hindu society has been since time immemorial. It is a queer mixture of the true and the untrue, fact and fiction, history and mythology; the result is a perverted logic and regressive recommendations. A few gems from the report: "the concept of divine origin of the caste system has the authority of the holiest of Hindu scriptures"; "if religion was ever used as an opium of the masses, it was done in India"; "(shudra's) social labor was the life-blood of India's great civilization"; "the role of caste status was so pervasive in society that the idea and administration of justice were colored by it."

The extensiveness and intensity of the denigrate Hinduism project has been tremendous. Few intellectuals have recognized the fact that the history of India has been the history of assimilation. As Communist Party of India leader Bhogendra Jha points out, "India has the tradition of assimilation; the West, of annihilation." Assimilation, of course, has not been in accordance with the principles of Voltaire, Rousseau, and Marx; but in India millions have not perished because of the iniquitous social system. Comparing this with the West's record in the Americas and Australia — where entire civilizations like those of the Mayas and the Aztecs were annihilated and peoples like the Red Indians and Aborigines had to face genocide — the Indian social structure can be called humane. But then the denigrate-Hinduism project ignores all these facts, as it is part and parcel of the liberal-Marxism-Gandhian idiom.

A few observations by AL Basham in his *The Wonder That Was India*, arguably the best book on ancient India, would show the hollowness of the denigrate-Hinduism project: ". . . our overall impression is that in no other part of the ancient world were the relations of man and man, and of man and the state, were so fair. In no other early civilization were slaves so few in number, and in no other ancient law book are their rights so well protected as in the *Arthashastra*. No other ancient lawgiver proclaimed such noble ideals of fair play in battle as did Manu. In all her history of warfare Hindu India has few tales to tell of cities put to the sword or of the massacre of non-combatants. The ghastly sadism of the kings of Assyria, who flayed their captives alive, is completely without parallel in ancient India. There was sporadic cruelty and oppression no doubt, but, in comparison with conditions in other early cultures, it was mild. To us the most striking feature of ancient Indian civilization is its humanity."

Devil Quoting Scriptures

Hindu-bashing has been a favorite pastime of Indian communists, Left-of-the-Centre academics, teenybopper intellectuals, and sundry other Left-libbers. They had a lot of fun at the expense of the state exchequer for decades. For, the Establishment was favorably disposed towards them and tried to keep them in good humor. Legitimacy and respectability were bestowed upon them during the Nehru era; Indira Gandhi built institutions to accommodate them with comfort. And they could have lived happily ever after, denigrating Hinduism even more vigorously, an exercise for which the liberal-Marxist-Gandhian shibboleths come so handy. But this denigration underwent a sea change by the end of the eighties.

For, the diabolical Hindu communalism had once again started raising its ugly head. This was the turning point. Leftist intellectuals realized that unrestrained and unsubstantiated Hindu-bashing would be counter-productive; it would only help the Hindutva brigade. Instead of going all-out against anything Hindu, they adopted a cautious approach. There was a strategic about-turn. Gone were the days of downright Hindu denigration, when it was fashionable to coin derogatory terms like the Hindu rate of growth. Now, Leftist intellectuals waxed eloquent about the greatness of Hinduism, its legendary tolerance, its mind-boggling diversity, etc. Various communist fronts swung into action. When the Ramjanmabhoomi-Babri Masjid controversy was at its peak, the fronts came up with slogans like *kan-kan mein vyape hain Ram, mat bharkao danga lekar unka naam* (Lord Ram is immanent in every particle, don't instigate communal riots in his name). The most important and high-profile of these fronts, the Safdar Hashmi Memorial Trust (Sahmat), launched a series of campaigns and programs to fight against the "communal forces" which were, and are, a threat to the "composite culture" of India. Suddenly, agnostic intellectuals started seeing great merit in the works of Sufi saints and Bhakti poets. Rootless Left-libbers, who never liked to speak Hindi, started relishing devotional poems in Brajbhasha, a dialect of Hindi. The *tamashas* organized by Sahmat, generously funded by the Establishment, acquired the status of a pilgrimage for Left-libbers.

This line of action was against Hindutva; at the same time, Leftist intellectuals propounded the theory that Hinduism and Hindutva were, and are, two different things. Ashis Nandy, who was associated with the Delhi-based Centre for the Study of Developing Societies, wrote an article in *The Times of India* with the self-explanatory title "Hinduism versus Hindutva: The Inevitability of a Confrontation" (18 February 1991). According to Nandy, "Hindutva will be the end of Hinduism. Hinduism is the faith by which a majority of Indians still live. Hindutva is the ideology of a part of the upper-caste, lower-middle class Indians, though it has now spread to large parts of the urban middle classes." Further, "Hindutva is one of those pathologies which periodically afflict a faith or a way of life. Hinduism has, over the centuries, handled such pathologies; it still retains the capacity to handle one more."

In other words, Hinduism is a great faith, a way of life which is resilient and timeless; Hindutva is a passing phase, a seasonal fever which comes and goes. Hinduism is noble; Hindutva, ignoble.

Beyond the sophistry lies the strategy: don't lampoon Hinduism; attack only Hindutva. For, then the votaries of Hindutva won't be able to allege that the Leftist intellectuals are anti-Hindu. It would be better to concentrate upon the aspects emphasizing the tolerance, pluralism, and diversity of Hinduism; glorify these aspects and shout from the rooftops that the Hindutva brigade is determined to do away with this glory; it wants to make Hinduism a monolithic religion, bulldoze Little Traditions, straitjacket all plurality, and prepare the human material for a fascist, Hindu Reich. Needless to say, the Leftist intellectuals were opposed to this Nazification; they found an icon in Gandhi and a useful medium in the liberal-Marxism-Gandhian idiom. So, when the Babri Masjid was demolished, one of their slogans was *Gandhi, hum sharminda hain, tere katil zinda hain* (Gandhi, we are ashamed that your murderers are still alive). The protagonists of Hindutva were responsible for the assassination of Gandhi as well as for the demolition, and the intellectuals were appalled to discover that the fascists had not been annihilated even after such sacrilegious acts. It seems that the irony of exhibiting the instincts of vengeance while remembering the prophet of peace has largely gone unnoticed. But then all is fair in the war against the votaries of Hindutva who want to Semitize Hinduism.

The Semitization line of argument was presented by some Leftist intellectuals at a time when the BJP was posturing aggressively and the Ramjanmabhoomi-Babri Masjid movement was at its peak. Interestingly, an axiom of the Semitization theory is that the Semitic tradition, with its stress on homogeneity, is inferior to the Hindu tradition which thrives on and promotes heterogeneity.

Many Leftist intellectuals started claiming that they wanted to keep Hinduism in its pristine form — with its plurality, diversity, etc. And, the argument went, the Hindutva brigade wants to defile the grandeur of Hinduism by Semitizing it. It was a curious situation: the traditional haters of Hinduism became its defenders — that too, against its traditional champions!

Appropriating the Gandhi Icon

The only thing permanent in the communist discourse seems to be the disdain for Hinduism. In general, however, their friends and enemies have changed. Take the case of Mahatma Gandhi.

These days Leftists show great respect for Mahatma Gandhi. Socialists like Jayaprakash Narayan, Jawaharlal Nehru, and Ram Manohar Lohia have always held Gandhi in high esteem. But communists and highbrows, English-speaking Left-libbers have not always been as favorably inclined towards him. It was only in the late eighties and the early nineties that their admiration for Gandhi increased considerably.

The most important reason for this is the rise of the star of Hindu nationalism on the political firmament. It is a simple case of enemy's enemy being a friend. The liberal-Marxist-Gandhian idiom is so prevalent, and political hypocrisy so deep-rooted, that even the Bharatiya Janata Party (BJP), the chief protagonist of Hindu nationalism, has started acknowledging the "greatness" of Gandhi. "In reality it is the Rashtriya Swayamsevak Sangh (RSS) and others inspired by the Sangh that have been perpetuating the legacy of Mahatma Gandhi by striving to fulfill his cherished dream of Ramrajya and swadeshi", said Rajendra Singh, head of the RSS. The report was carried in the *Organizer* (8 February 1998), the RSS mouthpiece. This despite the fact that Gandhi's ideology was the antithesis of Hindutva and his leadership a saga of deHinduization of the Congress and of the Indian polity. But the Left was intelligent enough to perceive the basic contradictions between Hindutva and Gandhism. It decided to appropriate the Gandhi icon for the fight against Hindutva.

It was not that communists always had a very high opinion about Gandhi. "The imminent collapse of Gandhism", thundered MN Roy in 1922, "will close a romantic and exciting chapter of Indian national movement. It will demonstrate that a socially revolutionary movement cannot be influenced by reactionary forces." In 1927, R Palme Dutt wrote, "The spiritually reactionary propaganda of Gandhism is an enemy of the interests of the masses." In 1931, he wrote, "Gandhism is already dying." In 1942, Dutt called Gandhi "the pacifist evil genius of Indian politics", and that "to all that is young and generous in India the name of Gandhi is an object of cursing and contempt, the name of Judas." Similarly, another communist leader, PC Joshi, too, wrote in 1942, "Gandhism is the path of negation. . . . The outlook of negation, the policy of passivity and the practice of subservience — this is Gandhism today."

All this changed with Gandhi's assassination on 30 January 1948. Dutt at once realized that Gandhi could be a useful ally. "Referring to Gandhi's efforts just before his death to quell communal violence, Dutt hinted at a new tactic — that Gandhi's martyrdom can be utilized by the Communists", wrote Gene D Overstreet and Marshall Windmiller in *Communism in India*. Dutt said that in his efforts for communal harmony, Gandhi had "worked in close association with the Communists. At the last Gandhi and the revolutionary working class began to find one another in the common fight for democratic unity of the people. . . . The need for democratic unity of the left is greater than ever. The democratic forces of India will carry forward the fight to see that Gandhi's death shall not be in vain, that the fight shall go forward to the victory to true independence and democratic unity for India".

Gradually, the communists' attitude towards Gandhi softened, a process in which the eminent leader EMS Namboodiripad played a key role. According to Overstreet and Windmiller, "There were interesting indications by the middle of 1957 of a possible rapprochement between the Communists and *Bhoodan* (the Gandhian movement of land distribution). In April, just a few months after the Communists formed their government in Kerala, Vinoba Bhave entered the state on a 54-day walking tour. Communist Chief Minister EMS Namboodiripad journeyed to the border to receive Bhave and the two had long private talks. Namboodiripad also attended one of Bhave's prayer meetings and asked the *Bhoodan* leader to autograph one of his books for him. . . Bhave. . . appealed to his *Bhoodan* workers to make the people understand that communism and socialism, like the Jumna and Ganges rivers, could join together in the ocean of *Sarvodaya*." Similarly, the CPI mouthpiece, *New Age* wrote, "The fact that people of the stature of Acharyaji [Bhave] are criticizing the CPI, and constructively too, is not only welcome but demonstrates that Communists are no more than a 'splinter group determined to create trouble,' but a party strong enough and with its roots firmly in the Indian people."

The rapprochement between Gandhism and communism grew as the liberal-Marxist-Gandhian idiom gained currency and respectability. It came of age when realization dawned in the early nineties that the BJP's rule over the country was a distinct possibility. This led to the lionization of Gandhi as the foremost secular hero. His "spiritually reactionary propaganda," his "outlook of negation," "policy of passivity" and "practice of subservience" — everything was forgotten, rationalized, or glossed over. He was hailed as a great leader who, though deeply religious personally, stood for inclusivism, plurality, and tolerance. Gandhi was abstracted and then appropriated by the Left. He ceased to be a philosopher or leader; he was reduced to an icon — the secular icon. According to a pamphlet distributed by the Safdar Hashmi Memorial Trust (Sahmat), the most high-profile communist front, "Gandhi was anathema to the votaries of Hindutva because of his grand strategy of uprooting the rule of foreigners. He had rightly calculated this would not be possible unless all Indians joined in the endeavor, regardless of class, religious faith, caste or region. Indeed, this is why Gandhi turned the freedom fight into a mass movement, a characteristic that was to become so important in conceiving post-British India as a republican democracy. This is why the RSS and the similar outfits hated him."

So, in the secularist narrative, Gandhi is the warrior hero, his assassination the worst possible sin, and the votaries of Hindutva diabolical forces.

The Political Economy of Art

Leftist artists were sharp enough to realize that the war against diabolical Hindutva forces can be a rewarding engagement. Let's see how.

In his film *Sardari Begum*, director Shyam Benegal makes a statement which is eloquent in silence. In the movie, the protagonist, Sardari, is fatally hit by a stone in a communal riot. As the riot intensifies, and is covered in a long shot, a flag of the Bharatiya Janata Party (BJP) makes a sudden appearance. The message is unambiguous: the communal Hindutva brigade is behind all trouble. Not only that, it is also responsible for the assault on — what is known as — our "composite" culture, which is personified in Sardari who sings *ghazals* as well songs of Krishna and Radha.

Showing the BJP flag was not germane to the theme of the movie; it seemed contrived, an unnecessary interpolation. But then these are the days of militant secularism; one has to flaunt one's secular credentials in an unabashed manner; and the best way to do is to denigrate the BJP. Of course, there are other, less direct ways of doing the same; for instance, people in khaki can be shown fomenting trouble. Benegal, however, is a shrewd director. He knows that by directly hitting the biggest political party he would earn more applause from the intellectual-cultural elite which is predominantly Leftist and, therefore, secular.

This is an incestuous coterie. All art, culture, literature, and intellectual discourse remain within the domain of this coterie; they have to conform to a paradigm which is defined by the coterie; any attempt to escape the prison-like domain is punished ruthlessly. So, eminent classical dancer Sonal Mansingh was censured because she had accepted to perform at a function organized by the Vishwa Hindu Parishad; that was in the wake of the demolition of the Babri Masjid on 6 December 1992.

The coterie. The same faces appear everywhere — at the Kamani Auditorium, the Shri Ram Centre of Art and Culture, and the Triveni Kala Sangam in New Delhi, at the art galleries, in seminars, at the *tamashas* organized by the Safdar Hashmi Memorial Trust (Sahmat). The same names appear in newspapers and magazines; the same people appear on television. The same people commend, criticize, and comment on each other. There are intrigues, backbiting, and bickering; but when the issue is secularism there is unanimity. Anybody who doesn't fall in line is dealt with firmly.

Maqbul Fida Husain painted Saraswati, the goddess of learning, in the nude. Many Hindu organizations objected to this; the BJP was one of them; its leader, KR Malkani, was one of those who denounced Husain. Not surprisingly, the coterie stood firmly behind Husain. A prominent Leftist historian, Harbans Mukhia, wrote in *The Pioneer* (18 October 1996):

Whenever Husain drew inspiration from a mythology for his art, which has been frequent, it was Hindu mythology. Whenever he painted any figure from a religious stream, it was the figures of Ganesh, Durga, Saraswati.

So immersed is he in this religio-cultural stream and so definitive is his own identification with it and of it with the essence of Indianness, that there is never a trace of self-consciousness of a Muslim artist's representation of Hindu mythological figures in these paintings. . . .

But for all this he clearly cannot be forgiven by the Bajrang Dal and Mr [KR] Malkani for bearing a Muslim name, which in their eyes becomes the unitary definition of his being. All complexities, ambiguities, subtleties dissolve before the stark clarity of a Muslim name.

Mr Malkani does, however, prescribe a step to Husain to redeem himself if only in part: paint women from Muslim mythology and religious history in the nude. . . .

On the face of it, Malkani's prescription seems to be communal and obnoxious; but isn't it a fact that had an artist or a writer taken similar, or even much less, liberty with Islam, his fate would have been similar to that of Salman Rushdie.

There is nothing wrong in making the Right to Freedom of Expression absolute and allowing everybody to write, draw, or paint anything he or she wants to. But this right can't be with "reasonable restrictions" in some cases and without them in others. Leftists are quick to refer to Article 19 of the Constitution, which defines the Right to Freedom of Expression, whenever controversies like the nude Saraswati erupt. But it's a fact that some very prominent Leftist intellectuals had sought a ban on the writings of Right wing journalists Girilal Jain and Swapan Dasgupta. Similarly, Leftist students of the Delhi-based Jawaharlal Nehru University protested against the depiction of falling sickle and hammer in the James Bond movie *Golden Eye*. There was also a demand to ban the popular TV serial, *Chanakya*, because in it ancient, Hindu India was glorified in a melodramatic manner and saffron was — even iiterally — conspicuous by its presence.

Most of the Leftists are atheists or agnostics. This makes them particularly hostile to Hinduism; for here the Macaulayan disdain for anything native combines with the Marxian scorn for religion. As it is, Hindu society, in its scheme of things, is oppressive, repressive, and regressive. On top of that, if the Hindu polity is made Hindu-centric — which the BJP wants to do — the consequences would be calamitous. The campaign against Husain was seen as part of a conspiracy by the votaries of Hindutva — a conspiracy, as an eminent journalist of liberal-Left orientation wrote in a national daily, to create a "climate of intolerance and hatred for the Muslims".

A very important aspect of the controversy has gone unnoticed, namely the fanaticism of the secularists. Now, this appears to be an outrageous assertion, as fanaticism is assumed to be the monopoly of the "communal forces". So, how can the antithesis of communalism be accused of fanaticism?

Leftists and secularists are afflicted with what post-modernism calls logocentrism; they are obsessed with the post-Enlightenment concern for totality. In their scheme of things, there is little space for plurality or for the others — especially those who don't blindly believe in Western ideas and ideals. Hindutva, obviously, is an abominable threat to the Enlightenment project. Similarly, since spiritualism and religious beliefs do not fit into the framework of Enlightenment, they have no merit. Those who worship God or gods are under the spell of "false consciousness". (This is a curious term which often appears in Leftist discourses. The users are the most arrogant, self-righteous, and sanguine people. They talk about "false consciousness" as if there were unanimity among all philosophers what "true consciousness" is. The fact, though, is that no two philosophers — since the age of Socrates, Plato, and Vedic seers — have agreed on the nature of consciousness.) Leftists don't believe in any kind of divinity, but they do believe in their divine right to denigrate the religious beliefs of Hindus. Hence the self-righteous, secular fanaticism.

This fanaticism could be economically profitable for the enterprising spirits and imaginative minds. Remember the exhibition organized by Sahmat after the demolition of the Babri Masjid? In one of the exhibits, it was shown that Ram and Sita were siblings. The myth of Ram has hundreds of versions, the most famous being those of Valmiki, Sant Tulsidas, and Ramanand Sagar. Scholars discuss various versions at academic meets. But the Sahmat exhibition was not an academic affair; it was held in the full media glare. Union Human Resources Development Minister Arjun Singh was generous in giving grants to the organizers. They were hard-bent to prove that the Hindu nationalists wanted to destroy the "composite" culture of India, demolish the "little traditions" (as the Sangh Parivar had objected to the depiction of Ram and Sita as brother and sister), and impose monolithic, brahminic values.

In other words, it was a typical Sahmat *tamasha*, and such a *tamasha* is always an engaging affair. In it the presence of the coterie is mandatory; for, it is a secular cultural gathering *par excellence*. Here one can enjoy bhajans along with Sufi songs. There is a surreal tinge in the scenario: the thoroughly Westernized elite discuss the finer points of the Bhakti and Sufi movements; the agnostics talk sympathetically about the common features of the two religious movements; the deracinated intellectuals discuss folk culture.

In the controversies mentioned above, and other similar ones, there is a pattern: rub the "communalists" the wrong way and gain publicity, for the voluble Left will support you blindly if you play your cards deftly. The same happened in the *Tamas* case during Rajiv Gandhi's rule. The Govind Nihalani film, based on the eponymous novel by Marxist writer Bhishm Sahni, obliquely suggested that it was mainly Hindu and Sikh fanatics who were behind the sanguinary riots during Partition. As expected, Hindu and Sikh organizations strongly protested — and the Leftists equally strongly supported the film. In the process, Nihalani got free publicity.

Ditto with the *Fire* film controversy. The gay partners in the movie were named Radha and Sita. Deepa Mehta, the director, became a household name, though before the movie she was hardly known outside the coterie. The name of the game is: provoke. Provoke the saffron brigade and gain free publicity.

It Isn't Clever, But Isn't It Art?

One often comes across a small painting on the back of an autorickshaw or truck. It's a landscape — a mountain, a lake, a tree, a few spots which are supposed to represent birds. Nothing in the painting has any merit: the drawing is bad; the color composition is poor; the pattern is jejune. It's a bad work of art — yet, a work of art it is.

Now, if cinema is a form of art, every film is a work of art. It doesn't matter whether the director is Satyajit Ray of Manmohan Desai; it may be good cinema or bad cinema, but as long as it is cinema, it's a work of art. So, what this hiatus between "art" films and "commercial" movies?

At the heart of the hiatus lies the inveterate arrogance of Leftist intellectuals. "They" — the Raj Kapoors and the Vijay Anands, the Prakash Mehras and the Subhash Ghais — sell sex and violence, melodrama and cheap sentimentalism, regressive values and aggressive jingoism to the masses. "We", say the Shyam Benegals and the Govind Nihalanis, are the champions of social realism. "They" sacrifice "art" at the altar of "commerce"; "we" are concerned with "art" for the masses.

The problem with the masses, however, is that they find "art" cinema utterly boring, notwithstanding the film critic and the highbrow. The masses are hooked to the "all-pervasive Bollywood variety of film", wrote Adoor Gopalakrishnan in the *Frontline* (22 August 1997). These movies are "designed and executed for popular consumption and always trying to cater to an untrained kind of taste or logic." Since the masses have "an untrained kind of taste" and a perverted "logic", the movies meant to cater to their choice cease to be works of art. Hence they are "formula" or "masala" movies, "run-of-the-mill cinema." They have to be banished from the world of art by the cultural-intellectual coterie. As a natural corollary, the rest becomes "art" cinema.

Several issues are involved in this neat categorization of "art" cinema and "commercial" cinema. First, why do the subalterns reject the former? The champions of "art" cinema are unambiguous on this point: the masses have "an untrained kind of taste." But whose responsibility is it to build the bridge between a work of art and the audience? Shouldn't the artist reach out to the viewer through his work? He should, but the problem here is that the "art" film-maker has a different audience to address to — the coterie: this is the audience he has chosen;

this is the audience that gives him recognition and arranges, directly or indirectly, his finances. If the masses lack the aesthetic sense to appreciate his cinematic genius, too bad for them. The art film maker knows his de Sica and Fellini and Eisenstein; he won't come down from his pedestal. His cinema is what the People *ought* to appreciate; for that the people have to be People as seen in the TV serial *Nukkad*: the People who are inherently good, bereft of any religious strife, caste prejudice, and regional bias, free from the spell of "false consciousness." Unfortunately, such People (who should ideally be the audience of the "art" film-maker) exist only in his imagination; so, he settles for the coterie. His cinema remains "cinema with a purpose", a cinema that is "uncompromising in its attitude." (This also explains why not a single worker or landless peasant is able to appreciate the works of Leftist painters, even if some of the artists have been communist party members. The workers' idea of art is confined to calendar paintings which are so much scoffed at by Leftist intellectuals)

The Leftist film-maker banishes "commercial" cinema and finds "art" cinema to be confined to the coterie — for "art" cinema is of, for, and by the coterie. He does not like the situation; what particularly pains him is that, as Gopalakrishnan wrote, "Indian cinema. . . came to mean, by and large, commercial cinema, which was generally accepted as 'mainstream cinema'." This was indeed a diabolical development. For, "they" do "commercial" cinema; they are *banias*, *lalas*, worshippers of Mammon. How can "they" defy "our" diktat of banishment and claim to be the "mainstream"? Only "we" can do cinema which is "art" cinema; "we" are artists, committed people, agents of change.

Though the arty film-maker does not shed his anti-Establishment pretensions, a conspicuous feature of "art" cinema is that it is funded by government agencies; often it is shown tax free. It was "art" cinema and its champions who bagged all the National Awards for a number of years. Film critic Anil Saari was quoted in *The Pioneer* (13 May 1998): "The talented Rakhee's wonderful performance in the experimental *27*

Down didn't fetch her an award. After all, she was from the mainstream, you see. Also the brilliant Jaya Bhaduri, whose caliber was universally acknowledged and admired in the seventies, never got a look-in for the same reason. It looked like a private, Old Boys Club comprising a coterie of arty film makers whose job was to milk the government exchequer, not give a damn about their audience and laugh all the way to the bank."

The *Pioneer* article was published in the wake of Karishma Kapoor's getting the National Award for her performance in *Dil To Pagal Hai*. The coterie had raised a hue and cry, but it was not for the first time. The author of the article, Manojit Lahiri, wrote: "Wherever a heavy-duty star from the mainstream. . . scooped an award — Rekha in *Umrao Jaan*, Amitabh in *Agneepath*, Sunny Deol in *Ghayal* — all hell broke loose. Howls of protest emanated from purists. How dare these guys with their vulgar, escapist, superficial and regressive fare be allowed into this hallowed territory? They should stick to their glitzy, hyped, masala-specific awards ceremonies. Let them remain informed that the National Awards celebrate excellence in if a cinema, performance and sensibility that is alien to them. So they should get lost — and stay lost."

A member of the coterie was quoted by Lahiri as saying: "My God, is nothing sacred? Having corrupted the sensibilities of the youth, Bollywood, the sole manufacturer of opium for the masses, now must be laughing its head off. The impossible has happened! One of their 'tinny' stars of a mass-targeted mindless musical kitsch has picked up one of the nation's most prestigious awards, sidelining, undoubtedly, several worthier talents from anti-glamour, pro-realism 'other' cinema. Shameful! To me, this marks a new low. From now on, I shall treat the National Awards as a huge joke." In the same vein, the noted critic Amita Malik said: "While I have nothing against Bollywood or mainstream cinema, I do genuinely believe that its induction and presence in the National Awards scenario is not quite sync with the philosophy, thinking or objectives of the body. The subjects, the treatment, the concerns — Bollywood represents a kink of cinema that goes totally against the very basics of what is propagated here. It's not a question of good or bad but whether it is appropriate or compatible. It's not."

The effort has always been to banish "mainstream cinema." The best example of this is the *Oxford Book of World Cinema*, in which Ashish Rajadhyaksha wrote on Indian cinema. If somebody doesn't know anything about Indian cinema and he picks up the Oxford book, after reading Rajadhyaksha's account he would think the Indian film world means Satyajit Ray, Mrinal Sen, Ritwik Ghatak, Kumar Shahani, Mani Kaul, Shyam Benegal, and Govind Nihalani. For, it is mainly such people who have dominated the section on Indian cinema. The reader may think that these are the household names in the country. Dev Anand, Suraiya, Dilip Kumar, Madhubala, Vyjyantimala, Nutan, Ashok Kumar, Kishore Kumar, K Asif, KL Sehgal, SD Burman, Naushad, BR Chopra, Meena Kumari, Mohammad Rafi, Lata Mangeshkar, Asha Bhonsle, OP Nayyar, Raj Khosla, Vijay Anand, Chetan Anand, Kamal Amrohi, Prakash Mehra, Manmohan Desai — the list of the Bombay film world's great names is long indeed. But all these people are either not mentioned or occur as a passing reference. The same with a number of milestones of the Indian cinema. However, a paragraph is devoted to Mani Kaul's movies, watching which is a torture even for the most patient connoisseurs of cinema.

Rajadhyaksha's story of Indian cinema is like a history of Indian cricket in which Sunil Gavaskar and Kapil Dev are mentioned casually and chapter after chapter is written on players like Vikram Rathore and Brajesh Patel; or a book on the Mughal period in which 150 pages are written on Dara Shikoh, but Aurangzeb is dismissed in a footnote; for the former was secular and tolerant, while the latter was communal and intolerant.

Given a choice, the coterie would banish the "mainstream" cinema, as one of its members did in the Oxford book. At least, it could have kept the real thing — i.e., the "art" cinema — immune from the contagion of "masala" movies. As Amita Malik said, "Let them ['commercial' film makers] do their thing and their own glamorous award shows and leave the National Awards to a cinema dedicated to magic not merchandise."

In other words, Art shall remain Art and Commerce rot as Commerce, and the twain shall never meet. It is another matter that they have met quite often — Smita Patil dancing in the rain with Amitabh Bachchan in a Prakash Mehra film, Shabana Azmi working for Manmohan Desai, Girish Karnad for Dev Anand, Kulbhushan Kharbanda for the Sippys. And most of the times, Art has moved to Commerce, not the other way around.

Dialectical Duplicity

In the aftermath of Pokhran-II, communist leaders and Leftist intellectuals demonstrated their considerable skills in spreading misinformation and lies. Their reaction to the nuclear explosion by India on 11 May 1998 gives a fair picture of the techniques used by them for propaganda and hegemony.

As India crossed the nuclear Rubicon, Leftists cried hoarse about "jingoism", "chauvinism", and "ultra-nationalism". Even before that day, they had left no stone unturned in misleading the nation regarding its security concerns. They were quite successful in the fifties and the early sixties: 1962 was the denouement. They were also successful in preventing the country's nuclearization, thanks to the tremendous influence they exercised in the opinion-making apparatus. Therefore, the BJP government's decision to go nuclear was a great shock to them.

But our comrades did not give up. They kept on parroting the same old slogans and present the same fallacious arguments. The most important of them was the endeavor to create a fear-psychosis among people regarding economic sanctions. N Ram, editor of *Frontline*, wrote in the issue of 5 June 1998, that "at a minimum, *the immediate combined effect of the sanctions is likely to be serious for an economy that faces difficulties*. The markets have reacted in a somewhat panicky way; the rupee is weaker than it was before the explosions; there are indications that the cost of foreign funds may shoot up; and so on." Another anti-bomb crusader, Praful Bidwai, wrote in *The Times of India* (6 June 1998): "Even if the impact of direct sanctions is limited, multilateral loan delays/cancellations could be hurtful. Worse would be the downgrading of credit ratings and loss of investor confidence."

Interestingly, these were the people who were earlier fanatically exhorting the nation to beware of the World Bank, the International Monetary Fund (IMF), the World Trade Organization (WTO), intellectual property rights, multinationals, etc; for them these organizations and devices were meant to spread "neo-imperialism." Now, they were concerned about "the downgrading of credit ratings and loss of investor confidence."

In fact, the struggle against American hegemony and "neo-imperialism" has been the leitmotif of the Leftists of all hues; they had led many a phony war against US imperialism and attacked the West so many times with the ammunition of empty rhetoric and worn-out shibboleths. Yet, now they were supporting the solitary superpower on the nuclear issue — which, incidentally, is the top item in the American agenda. Leftists became allies of the West. And they did not see anything immoral or incorrect in it. The Left is always right. The Left is right when it is opposing the US, and it is right when it is supporting it.

Another Leftist argument that was doing the rounds was like this: with so much poverty and illiteracy in the country, it makes little sense to take pride in being a nuclear state. The fallacy of the argument lies in the fact that there is no link between nuclear bombs and poverty; bombs are not made at the expense of the downtrodden; and had India not made nuclear bombs, its progress in the direction of poverty-alleviation programs would not have been any better. In the wake of the Cold War, there was worldwide decline in arms expenditure; but the 'peace dividend,' about which pacifists so fondly pontificate, was nowhere in sight; there is no empirical evidence of the decrease in arms expenditure resulting in the welfare of the poor.

Many Leftists indignantly asked: "Why nuclear tests? Where is the threat?" This question was answered by Sushant Sareen, a political commentator, in *The Pioneer* on 21 May 1998. He argued that threat perception is a relative concept. Up until 1962, Jawaharlal Nehru, his Leftist advisors like VK Krishna Menon and many communist leaders did not think that there was a threat from China. Nestled comfortably in their beautiful ideological castle, and isolated from the heat and dust of realpolitik, they were sanguine in their belief that "socialist countries do not launch aggression." They went to the extent of ignoring the most convincing reports of Chinese mischief on our borders. When the government was grilled in Parliament about the territories grabbed by the Chinese in the Himalayas, Nehru made the famous statement that not even "a blade of grass grows" there (to which Mahavir Tyagi, a Congressman and former Defence Minister, retorted sarcastically, "Nothing grows here [pointing to his bald head]. Should we hand it over to the Chinese?"). There are not many instances in history when a head of government has so ardently and blindly shielded the belligerence of an enemy nation — that, too, at the cost of national interests. But it was the humility of Nehru that he later accepted his mistake.

CPM leaders and pro-CPM intellectuals, however, don't have any respect for bourgeois virtues like humility. Nor do they have anything to do with old-fashioned concepts like nationalism and patriotism; they know only of "ultra-nationalism" and "jingoism", "fascism" and "chauvinism". So, they don't find anything treacherous or immoral in doing public relations work for Red China.

According to media reports, China has spent millions of dollars in the US for lobbying — and the money was well-spent, President Bill Clinton being one of the indirect beneficiaries. Not surprisingly, their interests are taken care of at the highest levels, with the White House turning a blind eye on the misdemeanors of China, whether it was violation of human rights, state support to the barbarous trade in human organs, brazen violation of the missile technology and fissile material transfer regimes, and supply of sophisticated arms to Pakistan. There is no Sino-Pak nexus, thundered our communist leaders and Leftist intellectuals. This despite the information gathered by the Ministry of Defence, reports of intelligence agencies of India and other countries, and investigative stories published by *The Washington Post*. Obviously, the millions spent by China for lobbying in the US were paying dividends. But, in India, it didn't have to hire any professional publicist — pro-CPM intellectuals offered free service admirably. (Or, was it really free?). All in the name of disarmament, world peace, good relations with neighbors, and what have you. Never before was treason more glorified and hallowed, or patriotism more defiled and derided.

It seemed that the Leftists had lost all sense of proportion in the aftermath of Pokhran-II. Bidwai wrote in *The Times of India* (15 May 1998):

> The fact that a minority government — led by a party with 25 per cent of the vote — which lacks the democratic mandate to effect a fundamental, far-reaching change in long-established policies, conducted Pokhran-II only compounds its gravity.

By this line of argument, no government in free India has got any right to do anything, because 50 per cent mandate was never achieved by any party. As for the major decisions taken by minority governments, there were quite a few precedents: Indira Gandhi declared war on Pakistan when her minority government was supported by the Communist Party of India; VP Singh announced the implementation of the Mandal Commission Report without even informing his allies.

Some of the arguments offered by Leftists were so ludicrous that only the gullible could take them seriously. Denying existence of any Sino-Pak nexus in the face of a mountain of evidence, the Leftists went to the extent of saying that "Sino-Pakistani arms and technology deals have been hyped up. But as anyone familiar with recent Sino-Indian talks will testify, China offered to sell us the very same nuclear and missile components Pakistan bought!" (Bidwai in *The Times of India*, 6 June 1998). In other words, it was just business. There should have been no hard feelings. Yet, if India felt so bad, too bad for it. The peaceniks like Bidwai do not have any problems if China sells or promotes nuclearization. China does nuclear testing, no problem; Pakistan goes nuclear, no problem. But if India tests bombs at Pokhran, all hell is let loose by them.

There are any number of Leftists who still pursue the CPM line on Sino-Indian ties. According to them, it was India, and not China, which was in the wrong in 1962. In their scheme of things, there is nothing mischievous in China grabbing thousands of miles of Indian territory, not respecting the international border, not recognizing Arunachal Pradesh as part of India; there is nothing improper in China arming Pakistan to the teeth, aiding and abetting insurgency in North-Eastern states, and using Burma as a base for anti-India operations. China is not an enemy or even a potential threat. But any government with even an iota of commonsense and the slightest regard for empirical evidence cannot afford to give any credence to such a queer mixture of gibberish and rubbish. And it would never strike a sensitive defence deal with an adversary which is as inscrutable as it is unscrupulous.

Communists on Indian Nation

The friends of China in India are also as inscrutable and unscrupulous as the rulers in Beijing. Sitaram Yechuri, a politburo member of the CPM, appeared in Zee TV's program *Aap Ki Adalat*, in February 1997. What made the program significant was Yechuri's persistent effort to evade questions pertaining to the India-China war of 1962. Despite relentless quizzing by Manoj Raghuvanshi, the anchor, the CPM leader did not come out with any criticism of the Chinese aggression. This must have convinced any Indian nationalist that the communists are like the Bourbons of yore: they have learnt nothing and they have forgotten nothing.

There is no point in repeating the charges that are often hurled against the Indian communists — that they have been found in the enemy camp at the crucial moments of India's history, whether it was 1942 or 1962. Arun Shourie, in his well-researched book, *The Only Fatherland: Communists, Quit India and The Soviet Union*, has convincingly portrayed the traitorous role of the CPI during the 1942 movement. Communists not only collaborated with the British but were also proud of their treachery and were keen to impress upon the government of their niggardly role. To prove that the communist betrayal was real, and not a myth created by "bourgeois propaganda," Shouri has provided documentary evidence. Therefore, one feels that it will be more worthwhile to scrutinize the communists' perception of Indian nation before justifying or denouncing their activities during the Quit India movement and the Chinese aggression.

Right from the beginning, the communists, a few exceptions apart, have been the most Westernized lot — to the extent that their Westernization has amounted to de-Indianization. The fascination for Western concepts has been so great that the Indian communist theory has often neglected the basic facts about the country. Bhogendra Jha, a veteran communist leader from north Bihar, says:

> We try to conceive a nation according to Western definitions. But the fact is that the history of India is the history of assimilation. The Aryans came and settled here, and so did the Greeks, the Shakas, the Kushanas, and others. This uniqueness was beyond the comprehension of the West which is familiar with annihilation — e.g., of the Red Indians in America and the Aborigines in Australia. But there was a thread of cultural integration in India; for instance, by establishing four *mathas* in different parts of the country, Shankar underlined this unity.

Jha's problem is that he keeps in touch with the people — the real people, not the People as they *ought to be* according to Marxian philosophy — and with the tradition, ethos, and culture of the country. He is among the few communists who fought against the British during the Quit India movement. (Interestingly, this fact is ignored even by the Leftist historians who otherwise take great pains to justify the CPI's ignominious and traitorous role in 1942. For them, Jha, who talks about Indian tradition and culture, remains anathema, an outsider who does not put empirical evidence into the straitjacket of ideology, who is not de-Indianized enough to be trusted). Not surprisingly, Jha's interpretation is at variance with the mainstream communist historiography. The established canon owes a lot to Soviet theoreticians and historians like AM Dyakov who wrote in 1948 that in India there were a number of large *peoples*, each of whom no less numerous than the English, the French, or the Italians; that these *peoples* were distinguished by their individual culture, language, literature, etc. The multinational character of India was considered an axiomatic truth in the Soviet Union. In 1925, Stalin told a band of communist trainees in movements in Asia, "Now, India is talked about as one entity. But there can be hardly any doubt that in the case of a revolutionary upheaval, many hitherto unknown nationalities, each with its own language and its own distinctive culture, will emerge on the scene."

Similar views were expressed by Sir John Seeley in 1883: "India is not a political name, but only a geographical expression like Europe and Africa." Long back, Metternich, the embodiment of reaction in the post-Napoleonic era, had described Italy as a "geographical expression." In 1988, Sir John Stratchey wrote that "there is not and never was an India, or even any country of India, possessing, according to European ideas, any sort of unity, physical, political, social, religious; no Indian nation, no 'people of India,' of which we hear so much." The remarkable similarity between the views of reactionaries and revolutionaries, imperialists and supposedly anti-imperialists is not accidental; it is the result of Eurocentric assumption held by both sets of people. For them, it was a self-evident truth that a nation has to be defined "according to European ideas." And within this framework it is indeed impossible to define India as a nation. Since the Soviets had adopted the multinational definition of India, the *desi* communists followed suit and started parroting the line they were "advised" to adopt. Macaulayans as they were — Indian in blood and color, but European in taste, opinion, morals, and intellect — the Indian communists did not find anything objectionable in the multinational concept. In fact, they tried to rationalize it. So, Rajni Palme Dutt wrote in 1947 that "there are strong grounds for recognizing the multinational character of the Indian people." Even in the early forties, the communists had started propounding this view. As a consequence, they did not see anything wrong in Jinnah's two-nation theory. BT Ranadive said in August 1942 that the "Muslims in certain areas do form a distinct nationality." Another communist leader, Sajjad Zaheer, felt that "the demand of Muslim self-determination or Pakistan is a just, progressive, and national demand."

It was not just a question of the demand of Muslim self-determination. The communist mouthpiece, *People's War*, observed in 1942:

> To look upon the right of secession as the special fad of Jinnah, as the conspiracy of a few communalists to divide India in the interests of British imperialists, is to ignore the new Muslim awakening, as also of other nationalities, e.g., Andhra, Karnatakis. . . .

If there is no Indian nation, does it make any sense in talking about nationalism? Therefore, the communists did not feel any pangs of conscience when they played an anti-national role during the Quit India movement; many of them, like EMS Namboodiripad, still justify their ignominious stand of 1942. Nor did they have any qualms in supporting the two-nation theory of Jinnah; in fact, they elaborated that and developed it into a multinational concept.

The communists, used to seeing everything through Western blinkers, could never recognize the fact that India is more than a mere "geographical expression." True, India is not a nation "according to European ideas": there is no religion that binds all Indians; there is no ethnic or linguistic homogeneity; even political unity has been an exception rather than a rule in the entire history of India. Yet, the country has witnessed the evolution of a distinct *modus vivendi* which is unique in the sense that it accommodates a bewildering variety of social structures, philosophical systems, religious beliefs, and cultural patterns. India is a civilization; its language game has to be understood from within, as an insider, or at least without the prejudices and presuppositions of an outsider. Communists seldom had the patience or the inclination to become an insider and understand the country. In any case, what was there to understand? Didn't they know all, as they had read Marx (though, ironically, Marx had considered India a civilization)? Combining Marxian zeal to change the world with Macaulayan temperament, they propounded the multinational concept of India.

The theory persisted for a number of years even after independence, but gradually many among the communists started feeling uncomfortable with it. Ajoy Ghosh, in 1953, found that it was "not merely wrong but has disastrous implications which strike at the root of the unity of the toiling masses. . . ."

Perhaps the last time when the multinational concept triggered off a major controversy was in 1971. Sankar Ghosh wrote in *Political Ideas and Movements in India*:

> In October 1971, a sensation was caused in the country when it was reported that the CPM was considering afresh a proposal for the recognition of the multinational character of India and for the conferment on each nationality the right to secede from the Indian Union. Reference to this connection was made to the Marxist definition of nationality as enunciated by Stalin. . . . Promode Das Gupta, a CPI(M) leader, said that each nationality would naturally have the right of secession, but then he also said that it did not follow that such a right would be immediately exercised any more than the right of divorce meant that every marriage must necessarily be dissolved.
>
> This theory. . . gave rise to serious controversy within the country, and Promode Das Gupta soon had to issue a clarification saying that the formulation of this theory about the right of the nationalities in India would not, in fact, lead to secession.

Generally speaking, the fascination among the communists for the multinational concept has been directly proportional to their radicalism. Leaders of the CPI, derisively called Right communists by the super-Leftists, usually supported Indian foreign policy. They also opposed China's aggression in 1962. The more radical elements, who latter formed the CPM, were pro-Chinese during the Sino-Indian war. The extreme Leftists, or Naxalites, like Charu Mazumdar went to the extent of announcing their allegiance to Mao: "China's chairman is our chairman."

It is not surprising that whenever there is an issue concerning nationalism or patriotism, Leftists raise a hue and cry that jingoism is being promoted. When *Border* became a box office hit, and subsequently was exempted from entertainment tax, similar noises were heard. But it was *Roja*, a film by Mani Ratnam, which caused a lot of consternation among progressive circles. The movie was accused of promoting fascism. According to Rustom Bharucha in *In the Name of the Secular*, *Roja* needs to be seen in the context of growing fascistic tendencies in the country. He discusses "the 'manufacture of consent' by which the crisis in Kashmir is being circumvented by the government. Far from being a freak box office hit, the film has been made possible through the larger consent of the media culture surrounding it. In turn, it has contributed to this culture substantially by inscribing (and thereby, reinforcing) the official line on Kashmir with an illusion of reconciliation. Ultimately, Kashmir is 'ours,' sovereignty of its people a secondary issue to the territorial integrity of the state within the nation. After all, as out ministers across parties have unanimously declared, 'Jammu and Kashmir has been, is, and shall be an integral part of India'."

In other words, there was a conspiracy of colossal proportions to make *Roja* a hit in which the government left no stone unturned — it was exempted from entertainment tax — and the media collaborated willingly. In fact, the entire ruling class participated in the conspiracy, as the statement of the ministers clearly showed. In *Roja*, "the official position on Kashmir is validated in the larger endorsement of the film." To stress the point, Bharucha also mentions that the movie was recommended by LK Advani and TN Seshan. Page after page, the writer goes on arguing that *Roja* became commercially successful because it was an adroit exercise in the "manufacture of consent". But was it no more than that? Wasn't the story-line new, direction gripping, cinematography captivating, and music lilting? Of course, it was loud and unrealistic at places; undoubtedly, it was not the finest specimen of cinema; but it had enough ingredients to make it click at the box office.

In the Leftist scheme of things, no nationalist dimension was involved. "Not only is the hype surrounding the film directly related to public relations and big business, it has been orchestrated to enhance an integrationist image of Kashmir. . . . More disturbing than the rave reviews which have gushed about *Roja*, are those critiques which have self-righteously vindicated the patriotic premises of the film with a specious objectivity." In the ultimate analysis, "patriotic premises of the film" have no validity. But why were such premises, postulates, and sentiments received so well all over the country? An article in the Leftist *Economic and Political Weekly* (14 May 1994) answered this question:

> [This was a time] when the Hindu Right's rhetoric on Kashmir and Muslims was more strident than ever before, [coinciding] with the government's claim to have successfully solved the "Punjab problem". This was also the time of increased state repression in Andhra Pradesh, Assam, Bihar, Gujarat, tribal areas of Maharashtra, Madhya Pradesh and Kashmir itself. All these states (except Gujarat) apparently suffered from "terrorism" and the governments of the states and the centre were busy "tackling the extremist menace" with a variety of brutal, unconstitutional ways.

Two points in this passage deserve analysis. First, the identification of nationalism and patriotism (which is jingoism in Leftist parlance) with the "Hindu Right" — i.e., the Bharatiya Janata Party (BJP). And since anything related to the BJP is odious, reprehensible, and wicked, patriotism is at best a hoax and at worst a precursor to fascism. The identification of nationalism with the BJP and fascism goes down well with the theories on Indian nation propounded by British imperialists,

Soviet theoreticians, and Indian communists of the forties' vintage: if India is a "geographical expression", the fuss about Indian nationalism has to be part of a conspiracy. Hence the indignation at the "integrationist image of Kashmir". Hence there is no "terrorism" in Kashmir; there is only a freedom struggle, a movement for *Azadi*.

Second, the concepts Indian government, Indian state, and Indian nation are deliberately confused in Leftist discourse. Normally, the criticism begins with the condemnation of the armed forces which, it is argued, have a very poor record on the human rights front. Then it proceeds to the failure of the government — all those noises about 'state repression.' From here the criticism graduates to the Indian state. The final stage is that of the Indian nation — all its premises and postulates are challenged. It is not a linear progression; censure of the Indian government may follow the repudiation of the concept of Indian nation. Ultimately, this repudiation is the goal. Sophistry, chicanery, subterfuge — everything is done to achieve this goal.

History of a Lie and the Lie of History

If reality resembles a farce, what parable could be more appropriate than a joke? So, consider a joke-parable: A farmer took his cow to a fair to sell it. The fodder it needed every day was double any other cow would require; the milk it delivered was very little; and, on top of everything, its price was four times that of the best cows available in the fair. Puzzled, a prospective buyer asked the reason. The farmer replied, "Well, it has very good character." In Indian politics, secularism is like the character of the farmer's cow.

Why was the HD Deve Gowda government formed? Because all the honorable men and women wanted to keep the communal forces — i.e., the Bharatiya Janata Party (BJP) — out of power. You can embezzle public money, maintain illegal Swiss bank accounts, ignore national interests, treat ministries and government departments as your fiefs, kill people, rape women — everything is pardonable so long as you are secular. Hence

Laloo Prasad Yadav, Mulayam Singh Yadav, Taslimuddin, Phoolan Devi, Romesh Bhandari. In fact, about Bhandari no less a person than Deve Gowda said that though he (Bhandari) had made a hundred mistakes as a governor, he was secular. In other words, secularism is a miraculous, virtuous *parasmani* — whoever touches it starts glowing in the golden radiance of virtuousness!

This is not to suggest that everybody in the BJP is an angel; charges of corruption have been hurled upon its ministers in several states; and some of its allies are not exactly the best example of probity. Nor has the BJP provided, till the time of writing these lines, excellence in administration. It was because of incompetence, and worse, of the BJP governments in Madhya Pradesh, Rajasthan, Delhi, and Himachal Pradesh that they were voted out of power. People, many of them rank opportunists, defect from other parties to the BJP, and *vice-versa*. The BJP doesn't seem to be any worse than the Congress, the Janata Dal, and other parties. So, why does it have to face ostracism?

The ostracism was the result of a persistent and comprehensive indoctrination in which the Left played a key role. Hindu nationalism has been presented as a diabolical ideology which is the product of a few perverted minds. The foremost among Leftist intellectuals who champion this line of argument is Bipan Chandra. According to this well-known historian, a "characteristic various communal groups (during the British period) shared was their tendency to adopt pro-government political attitudes. . . none of the communal groups and parties, which talked of Hindu and Muslim nationalism, took active part in the struggle against foreign rule."

Chandra's line has found remarkable acceptance in Leftist circles and official history. It suited both the Congress, the ruling party for most of the time after Independence, and the Leftists: the Congress got all the credit of freeing the country; and Leftists were assured of patronage. Any number of commentators have written about the Hindu nationalists' lack of interest in the freedom movement; if anything, their role was only negative, directly or indirectly assisting the British. Safdar

Hashmi Memorial Trust (Sahmat), a communist front organization which is involved in propaganda work through cultural activities, brought out a pamphlet at its annual function in the first week of January 1998. It said, "Neither [Hindu nationalists nor the Muslim League] fought the British." The votaries of Hindutva "had always spewed venom against those engage in fight to the finish against British imperialist rule."

In Leftist historiography, view are sacred while facts are flexible. Conclusions don't follow facts; it's the other way around. Only such events are noted and those statements quoted which have a bearing on the conclusions which are the starting point of any inquiry. So, the Bipan Chandras always ignore the fact that a galaxy of leaders during the freedom struggle were Hindu nationalists. Most of the leaders believed that religion or spiritualism can't be separated from politics. Aurobindo Ghosh felt that only spiritualism can be the basis of the nationalist movement. Lokmanya Tilak ridiculed the Westernized Indians and hoped that "the stream of Hindu religion [would] flow through one channel." Further, "religion is an element of nationality." Bipin Pal was of the opinion that "the Mother is the spirit of India." Similarly, Lala Lajpat Rai was the president of the Hindu Mahasabha at its Calcutta session in 1925. Three years later, he presided over the UP Hindu Mahasabha Conference at Etawah. There were a number of other prominent leaders as well whose views and activities deserve to be called "communal".

Even if these leaders can be condemned as communal, fascist, reactionary, etc, one has to truly overstretch one's imagination to call them pro-British. For, it was Tilak who made that profoundly revolutionary statement: "Swaraj is my birthright and I will have it." Lala Lajpat Rai died because he was assaulted by the police in a procession. And few Congress leaders suffered as much in British jails as Savarkar did, the towering ideologue of Hindutva (he coined the term). Yet, Ashis Nandy, Shikha Trivedy, Shail Mayaram, and Achyut Yagnik have the effrontery to proclaim in *Creating a Nationality*: "Hindu nationalism does not have a long past in India."

The Leftists were able to malign Hindu nationalism by using the concept that those who mix religion with politics are regressive, communal elements. Muslim League leaders and the Hindu nationalists did it in the British period; so, both must be communal. But Hinduism is not a religion, at least not in the Semitic sense of the word. Hinduism is a matrix on which a variety of philosophical systems, religious beliefs, social structures, and cultural patterns thrive; it can't be fitted into the straitjacket of religion. It is obvious, for there is no Book, no God (despite a plethora of gods), no church, no canon, and no Pope. But the communists could not see it, obsessed as they were, and are, with Western ideas.

The Leftists have also attained soaring heights in propagating falsehood by equating Hindu revivalism with Hindu obscurantism. To be more precise, the equation is:

Hindu nationalism = revivalism = obscurantism.

If the BJP comes to power, we would go back to the bad old days of *Manusmriti* when the favorite pastime of the dominant upper caste men (remember the oh-so-bad White male in the West?) was to torment the shudras and oppress women.

One need not be an Arnold Toynbee to see that Hindu revivalism was the anti-thesis on Hindu obscurantism. All the great socio-religious reformers of the nineteenth century who sought to revive what was best in ancient India also fought tooth and nail against the evils of caste, superstition, illiteracy, and the oppression of women. The Arya Samaj can be taken as a paradigm. It was an extremely aggressive revivalist movement. Its contribution in promoting literacy, women emancipation, and economic betterment is second to none. It is not a coincidence that the regions where the Arya Samaj was prominent — Punjab, Haryana, western UP — are among the prosperous parts of the country. The communists cannot comprehend these simple facts because often their understanding of the West is also as superficial as that of India. Otherwise, they could have realized that the Renaissance, too, was a revivalist movement — even etymologically. It endeavored to revive the glories of the classical period, to revive the best, the noble, and the sublime in ancient Greece, and to do away, though cautiously, with the debilitating effects of the Dark Ages under Christianity. What resulted from this romance with the past was humanist philosophy, reason, the Age of Enlightenment. Similarly, the consequence of the revivalist movement in India was, to a large extent, the emancipation of women and the delegitimization of the worst features of caste. It is because of their supreme disdain for empirical evidence that the Leftists assert that Hindu revivalism is nothing but obscurantism.

But why and how are Leftists able to sway opinion in their favor, in spite of such obvious holes in their theories? Why do their hypotheses pass off as substantive theories and their theories as self-evident truths? The answer lies in the intellectual hegemony of the Left. This hegemony grew in magnitude after Independence, thanks to a set of fortuitous circumstances, which had no relation to the electoral strength of the Left.

Summary

This section contains discussions on a variety of subjects — from art and culture to the nuclear bomb. The reason is simple: the tools and techniques employed by the Left for hegemony are varied; their comprehensive scrutiny will not be possible without taking into account a lot of things. Thanks to apriorism, Leftists have been able to make unverifiable assertions and postulate preposterous theories, and convert the masses into the Masses. The denigrate-Hinduism project has helped them keep the Hindu nationalist ideas at bay. Art, culture, literature, and cinema having become a preserve of an incestuous coterie, this hallowed realm has been saved from any disagreeable influence. A kind of esthetic apartheid has been promoted by this coterie. All this happened quite smoothly, as all debates were conducted in the liberal-Marxist-Gandhian idiom. The climate of opinion that was built in the first four decades of Independence was such that it encouraged secular McCarthyism: most of the dissent was suppressed and the dissenters were demonized.

The Leftists have left no stone unturned in establishing and then maintaining their intellectual hegemony. No means were considered foul enough to refrain from. Thanks to the communists' doublespeak, Gandhi, once compared with Judas, has emerged as a great secular humanist. Hinduism, once disparaged for every real and fictitious evil, is now seen as a great religion. Nuclear explosions by India were condemned in strongest terms, but those by the erstwhile Soviet Union and China were applauded. Sophistry, prevarication, chicanery, duplicity — the Leftists have used everything to establish their intellectual supremacy.

CHAPTER 3

History of Indian Communism

We must at present do our best to form a class who may be interpreters between us and the millions we govern; a class of persons, Indian in blood and color, but British in taste, in opinion, in morals, and in intellect.   *Thomas Macaulay, 1835*

A Bird of Passage

The birth of the Communist Party of India (CPI) is shrouded in a controversy; and this controversy throws some light on the party, its leaders, and their mindset. It suggests that the Indian communist was, and is, before anything else, a hybrid of two civilizations, akin to genetic engineering.

It was the post-World War I period. There was a rise in prices and a slump in economic activity. Peasantry, the biggest section of the Indian population, was suffering from heavy taxation; the condition of workers was pitiable; and educated unemployment was increasing. During the War (1914-18), the Allies, including the British, had promised political reforms; but the promise was observed only in the breach. Instead, what India got was the repressive Rowlatt Act and the Jallianwala Bagh massacre. In such a context, many young Indians found Gandhian methods slow, inscrutable, and ineffective; they started looking for an alternative; and many of them found it in communism.

We can identify four trends from which individuals and groups in their search for new paths for the struggle of independence turned to scientific socialism and communism under the impact of the Great October Revolution," writes Gangadhar Adhikari in the Documents of the History of the Communist Party of India.

These four trends are the following:

1. Indian national revolutionaries operating from abroad in the period of the first world war. . . [such] as V Chattopadhyaya, M Barkatullah, MPBT Acharya, MN Roy, and Abani Mukherji.

2. National revolutionaries from the Pan-Islamic Khilafat movement who went abroad in the war period. . . . Mohammed Ali Sepassi, Rahmat Ali Khan, Ferozuddin Mansur and Abdul Majid and Shaukat Usmani.

3. [In the post-war period, the Ghadar Party] was revived by Rattan Singh and Santokh Singh. . . who in 1922 took the initiative to establish contacts with the Communist International.

4. [And] the most important trend was of the national revolutionaries in India itself — from the leftwing of the National Congress, the terrorist organizations, the Akali movement (especially, its Babbar Akali leftwing which was linked with the Ghadar Party). Individuals and groups from this trend — when disillusioned by Gandhiji's ideology of non-violent resistance. . . .

On 17 October 1920, MN Roy, a revolutionary terrorist who had imbibed Marxism in exile, formed a Communist Party of India at Tashkent with six others — Evelyn Trent-Roy (his wife), Abani Mukherji and his wife, Rosa Fitingor, Mohmmad Ali, Mohammad Shafiq, and MPBT Acharya. On December 15, three more people joined — Abdul Qadir Serhrai, Masud Ali Shah Qazi, and Akbar Shah. "The batch of the Muhajirs", according to Adhikari, "who joined the Military and Political School at Tashkent at the end of 1920 and some of whom joined the Communist Party of India formed there in October. . . in the beginning of 1921, proceed[ed] to Moscow where they all join[ed] the Communist University of the Toilers of the East." After receiving training at the university, and assured of help from Moscow, they attempted to re-enter India but were arrested and tried in a series of Peshawar Conspiracy cases (1922-27).

Meanwhile, Roy was trying to establish contacts with the nascent communist groups like those of Sripad Amrit Dange in Bombay, Muzaffar Ahmad in Calcutta, and Ghulam Hussain in Lahore. Similar but less successful attempts were made by Roy's rival Berlin group whose important members were V Chattopadhyaya, Birendranath Datta (brother of Swami Vivekananda), and Barkatullah. In May 1924, Muzaffar Ahmad, Dange, Shaukat Usmani, and Nalini Gupta were jailed in the Kanpur Bolshevik Conspiracy Case.

An open Indian Communist Conference was held in Kanpur from 26 to 28 December 1925, which was attended by 300-500 people. It was convened by Satyabhakta who, in the words of the eminent Marxist historian Sumit Sarkar, "proved very much of a bird of passage." Satyabhakta was not expelled from the party; the environment was made conducive to his exit.

For, Satyabhakta had committed the unpardonable sin of emphasizing concrete realities instead of philosophical abstractions and putting the nation before ideology. He was an Indian first and a communist next. Thus he formed the Indian Communist Party; when it was converted into the Communist Party of India, he quit. It all seems to be semantic hair-splitting; but it's not: what lies behind is an attitude. Satyabhakta did not want his party to be reduced to an organ of a worldwide movement, the Communist International (Comintern).

"The Indian Communist Party," he declared in June 1925, "is absolutely an independent body. Our relation with the Comintern is of the nature of mutual sympathy as followers of the same principle. We are not ready to tie our hands, nor do we want to take orders from others. No doubt we want to change the present system of Indian society and government according to the communistic principle but only with due respect to the conditions and mentality of Indian people." Singaravelu Chettiar, who presided over the Kanpur Conference, also echoed similar views: "Indian communism is not Bolshevism, for Bolshevism is a part of communism which the Russians have adopted. We are not Russians." Maulana Hazrat Mohani, chairman of the reception committee, too, said in his speech, "Our organization is purely Indian."

Satyabhakta was cleary the leader of the group which believed that Indian communism would be a product and function of "the conditions and mentality of Indian people." Ram Bilas Sharma, an eminent Leftist Hindi author, in his *British Rule in Indian and Marxism* writes, "The views of Satyabhakta were correct in those circumstances." However, Satyabhakta's stand was unacceptable to those who considered the Comintern to be the sole repository of all wisdom and communist parties all over the world to be its regional offices. The foremost among them was MN Roy. According to him, "Nothing could be more non-communistic than to say that the Indian working class will play its historical role in the struggle for national freedom and work out its salvation independently of the international proletarian movement." Though Roy did not attend the Kanput meet — he was not in India — his influence on Indian communists for a period of time was considerable. In any case, it was Roy's line of thinking which emerged victorious after the conference. He was so furious with the assertion that "we do not want to take orders from others" that he went on insinuating that Satyabhakta was a British agent. Vindicating Roy's stand, Adhikari also accused Satyabhakta of timidity and shallowness. Muzaffar Ahmad, too, disdainfully dismissed the Kanpur Conference as "an entirely childish affair." He felt that October 1920 — that is, when Roy started his racket in Russia — was "the real date of the foundation of the Communist Party of India."

Who was Satyabhakta, whose name always appears whenever the birth of communism is discussed but invariably in a passing reference? Born in 1896 at Bharatpur, Rajasthan, he got involved in revolutionary activities when he was a teenager, for which he remained on the watch-list of the intelligence department for two decades. Once he was injured while making a bomb. He also participated in the First Non-cooperation Movement. His house and bookshop were raided by the intelligence department several times; and some of his publications were confiscated. Satyabhakta was one of the pioneers who ardently propagated Marxian ideas and zealously organized workers' movement in India. "In 1930, he wrote a book called *Karl Marx* which was published in Patna," according to Sharma. "The background was that of the Meerut Conspiracy Case (1929-33). The communist conference in Kanpur was five years behind. [It was in this hostile context that] Satyabhakta once again expressed his commitment to communism."

Adds Sharma:

> He never fully agreed with traditional revolutionaries. Even when he came under the influence of communism, he never opposed the Congress as many communists had done in the past or still do it. . . . Often there is puzzlement in his thinking but there is no confusion in his sympathy for the working class. He steered many revolutionaries towards Marxism and mass movement — it was his historic importance.

And what was the "historic importance" of Roy? The party that Roy launched was no more than a joke. According to Sharma, "Roy had founded a communist party in Mexico and attended the Second Congress of the Comintern as its representative. Now, the Third Congress was to be held. Had that party been in existence it could have once again sent Roy as its representative. But that party had played its historic role by sending him once as its representative. Therefore, Roy needed another party. . . . In other words, the real problem was the representation of Roy." So, that was the *raison d'etre* of Roy's Communist Party of India.

It was not only Sharma who doubted the commitment and sincerity of Roy; any number of radicals hurled charges of insincerity, fraudulence, and embezzlement of funds against him. Saumyendranath Tagore, a leader of the Bengal Workers' and Peasants Party, went to Moscow in 1927. Writing about his experiences there in third person, he narrated an interesting anecdote:

[Ossip] Piatnitsky, the then General Secretary of the Central Committee of the Comintern, sent for Tagore and had a long talk regarding the work of the communists in India. It was evident from the talk that quite a different picture of the communist activities in India had been presented to the Comintern by MN Roy. Piatnitsky had an idea that there were hundreds of communists in India in those days. When Tagore told him about the actual number of communists in India in those days, which did not exceed more than a dozen, Piatnitsky was taken aback. He said that it seemed unbelievable, as Roy had reported the existence of hundreds of communists in India. Tagore told him in reply that Roy might have hidden these communists in the Himalayas, they were neither heard nor seen in India. It was also evident from the talk with Piatnitsky that the Comintern had given enormous sums to MN Roy for financing the communist movement in India. Tagore informed Piatnitsky that hardly any money had been received in India and the growth of the communist movement was tremendously handicapped due to the lack of money and literature.

According to Overstreet and Windmiller, "Tagore's two charges against Roy — that he had misappropriated funds and misrepresented the size of the Communist apparatus in India — are corroborated to some extent by British Intelligence sources." Another political activist, Jotin Mitra, wrote to Mohammed Sipassi, Roy's right-hand man in Europe:

You people do not realize our difficulties here. . . . The boss [Roy] and family are living as Princes. . . and the boys here — real, sincere workers — are starving. You hypocrites mean no business, you are simply exploiters. Your behavior has created such a bad atmosphere against you that now, except a few of us, *all* in the Punjab, UP, Bombay and Bengal are losing confidence in you.

So, we have two leaders, Satyabhakta and Roy. The former lived in the country, popularized Marxist ideas, converted nationalist revolutionaries to communism, organized the masses, wanted Indian communism to be strong and independent, and faced repression. Roy, on the other hand, most of the time lived sumptuously in Europe, indulged in intellectual masturbation, kept important bureaucrats of the Comintern in good humor but had nothing to do with the masses, wanted Indian communists to be puppets of Moscow; and when he came to India, managed to get money from the British government after some time through BR Ambedkar. Yet, it was not Roy but Satyabhakta who was marginalized in the communist movement. Even Adhikari, who admitted that the history of the CPI begins with the Kanpur Conference, staunchly defended Roy and tried to belittle the contribution of Satyabhakta.

Why was this so? What's wrong in, as Satyabhakta wanted, formulating party policies in tune with the ground realities, "with due respect to the conditions and mentality of Indian people"?

About the Cuban Revolution, French philosopher Jean-Paul Sartre said, "The originality of this revolution consists precisely in doing what needs to be done without attempting to define it by means of a previous ideology." In fact, "doing what needs to be done" is the success formula of any revolution — whether in Russia, China, or Vietnam. Nowhere were the ideas of scientific socialism implemented exactly as enunciated by Karl Marx: in Russia, Lenin added a new dimension to communism by emphasizing the vanguard role of the party; in China, Mao redefined communism by peasantifying it; in Vietnam, Ho Chi Minh interpreted Marx and Lenin in a different manner. And all these interpretations struck root because they were in accordance with the local economic, social, political, and cultural conditions. In short, ideology was acclimatized.

Indian communist leaders, however, preferred to loiter in the realm of abstractions. Notwithstanding leaders like Satyabhakta — who were marginalized in any case — Indian communists were unable to grasp ground realities. This seems paradoxical, as they claim to have close contacts with the masses. But the masses, as the Indian communist leaders see them, are bereft of any social, cultural, and civilizational content; they are mere abstractions. They are like the characters in the popular TV serial *Nukkad* — innocent, inherently good and noble, without any caste bias, religious prejudice, or any other parochial vice. The problem with such "masses" is that they exist only in third-rate TV serials. To understand the real masses, one has to identify oneself with the masses; at least, one should be able to empathize with them. Indian communist leaders were not able to do that, thanks to the British legacy which had made them intellectually and temperamentally un-Indian. They viewed the history, society, culture, and traditions of India as a European would do. At the heart of their rootlessness, there were two factors: the push factor, namely the Macaulayan syndrome; and the pull factor, namely the internationalism and abstractions of Marxism. The pull factor did away with whatever Indianness was left in communist leaders. Hence their escape from concrete realities to abstract fantasies, from nation to ideology. A natural corollary was an abject surrender to the diktats of Moscow. For, who else can interpret the ideology better than those who had successfully implemented it. And hence the irrelevance of Satyabhakta — a bird of passage.

Ostrichized from Reality

Nineteen hundred and twenty was the high noon of MN Roy's political career; for, he entered into a celebrated debate with none other than the great Lenin. It was about the role of bourgeois nationalists. The episode really indicates that the ostrich-like attitude of Roy and other communists was not a consequence but the cause of their dependence on Moscow. For, had they been really dependent on Moscow, Lenin's views on the role of national bourgeoisie would have been accepted without an iota of doubt.

Lenin felt that the liberation movements in colonies led by the national bourgeoisie were democratic in nature and "all communist parties must assist the bourgeois democratic movements in these countries." Roy, on the other hand, asserted that "the bourgeoisie even in the most advanced colonial countries, like India, as a class was not economically and culturally different from the feudal social order. Therefore, the nationalist movement was ideologically reactionary in the sense that their triumph would not necessarily mean a bourgeois democratic revolution." The role of Gandhi was the crucial point of difference. Lenin believed that, as the inspirer and leader of a mass movement, Gandhi was a revolutionary. Roy maintained that as a religious and cultural revivalist, Gandhi was "bound to be a reactionary socially, however revolutionary he may appear politically." Here, "bound to be" is the operative phrase. A fine example of deductive logic. But politics is more than logic. So, we have a successful revolutionary with his practical suggestion: Lenin insisting on the collaboration between Indian communists and the national bourgeoisie, as the former were not strong enough to fight British imperialism. And we have a freelance, high-flying revolutionary with his belief that there were two distinct movements — one led by the national bourgeoisie with its goal of political freedom sans economic equality and the other led by the toiling masses. The absurdity of Roy's thesis was later recognized even by the communists themselves. As there were scarcely any Marxists — let alone any Marxist movement — in India in 1920, SG Sardesai, a prominent leader of the Communist Party of India, wondered in 1956, "How on earth was a communist party in a subject country secure the leadership of its freedom movement from the outset?"

But when the bound-to-be logic prevails, even wild dreams appear to be impending scenarios. It was a consequence of Roy's total dependence on ideology. There was nothing he could learn from India. In his scheme of things, everything in India was rotten, disgusting, putrid: politics (what good could be expected from the "reactionary" Gandhi), society (the rigid caste system, oppression, inequalities, backwardness), religion (mind-boggling superstition, stupid rituals). He wrote in *India's Message* (1950):

> The fact that even in the twentieth century India is swayed by the naïve doctrines of Gandhi speaks for the cultural backwardness of the masses of her people. The subtlety of the Hindu

philosophy is not the measure of the intellectual level of the Indian people as a whole. It was the brain-child of a pampered intellectual elite sharing power and privileges with the temporal ruling classes. It still remains confined to the comparatively small circle of intellectuals who try to put in a thin veneer of modernism and represent nothing more than a nostalgia. The popularity of Gandhi and the uncritical acceptance of his antics as the highest of human wisdom knock the bottom off the doctrine that the Indian people as a whole are morally and spiritually superior to the Western. The fact is that the great bulk of the Indian people are steeped in religious superstitions. Otherwise, Gandhism would have no social background and disappear before long.

In other words, the masses, owing to their "cultural backwardness" and to the fact that they were "steeped in religious superstitions," were a problem; they were not as they ought to be according to the tenets of Marxism. Roy was very much for the revolution, provided the masses behaved, but they did not. He was aghast to see that the masses continued to get "swayed by the naïve doctrines of Gandhi." Only if the communists could choose the people they wanted to lead! Roy could have left the people on their own, but he could not suppress the instinct to play savior; in spite of the refusal of the Indians to conform to the diktats of the ideology, he wanted to redeem them. Roy and his comrades were incorrigible redeemers.

In 1923, they sought to organize Workers' and Peasants' Parties (WPPs) all over the country which were to act as legal fronts of an illegal communist party. (That the British authorities were not fooled by this strategy is another story). This decision was influenced by the orders of the Comintern. However, in the short span of four years (1926-30), WPPs came into being, grew tremendously, and faded into oblivion. In their growth, Roy's role was minimal, as he was away from the country.

The sudden rise and equally sudden dissolution of WPPs proves two points. First, the objective conditions were conducive to the existence and growth of a Left-wing movement. It was also the period in which the communist influence in trade unions increased dramatically. The role of SA Dange in Bombay is a case in point.

Second, the dissolution of WPPs at the behest of the Comintern underlined the priority of Indian communist leaders. It brings their mindset into sharp focus; for them, the party line and ideological purity were of far greater significance than contacts with the people. Thinking at the Comintern was influenced by non-India factors; but its implications on Indian communists were profound.

Sympathetic commentators have attributed the communist withdrawal from WPPs as a result of "Left sectarianism". Harsher critics may call it the result of the excessive dependence on Moscow. But it was as much a case of imported wisdom as of contempt for local experience.

Bandwagonism of the CPI

The only ism the Communist Part of India (CPI) has consistently followed — at least since Independence — is bandwagonism.

When the adventurism of BT Ranadive failed in the late forties, the radical elements in the CPI were marginalized for some time. They had hoped for a glorious communist revolution just after Independence. With the failure of the Telengana movement in Andhra Pradesh, the communists — or most of them — realized that the capture of power by means of arms was not within the realm of possibility. The alternative was to join the mainstream of parliamentary politics. This was also made possible by the comparatively benign nature of the Indian state.

This is not to say the Indian state had imbibed all the Gandhian ideas of non-violence and tolerance, that coercion had ceased to exist. Indeed, the communists faced repression: there were tortures and extra-judicial killings, trials and imprisonment. Yet, it was the resilience and uniqueness of Indian democracy that the people for whom the establishment of a dictatorship was a tenet of faith were accommodated and, with the passage of time, assimilated. Even under the British, the communists — unlike their counterparts in, say, Germany — never faced annihilation. (In fact, they collaborated with the colonial rulers for a long period during the Quit India movement). Compared to what the Red Army faced at the hands of the Kuomintang in China, Indian communists were handled with kid gloves. Unlike Chiang Kai Shek in China, the chief political executive here, Jawaharlal Nehru, was an ideologically kindred soul. And this fact created dissensions within the CPI which ultimately led to split in the party in 1964.

The bandwagonism of the CPI is the product and function of its leaders' lack of confidence. As a consequence, they sought shelter in ideology and rhetoric. Hence their blind obedience to Moscow in the yesteryears and bending backwards to the whims and fancies of Laloo Prasad Yadav in the recent past when he was an ally.

When India became independent, the communists welcomed this historic event. But Soviet pundit AM Dyakov wrote in *New Stage in India's Liberation Struggle* (1947), "[The CPI] did not immediately understand the treachery of the leadership of the National Congress and counterpoised its Right to its Leftwing as though the latter were a progressive one." Since the general mood in the Cominform was anti-Nehru, the Central Committee of the CPI in December 1947 followed suit and denounced PC Joshi's thesis that the new government could be influenced by popular pressure. Later, in February 1948, the Second Congress of the CPI lambasted the comrades for harboring "illusions that socialism may be achieved by constitutional means." At this Congress, the new-found militancy was symbolized by the crowning of BT Ranadive, who replaced PC Joshi, a moderate, as general secretary. Ranadive was a Don Quixote who thought that the revolution was possible, if not imminent. He did not have any understanding of the situation in Telengana in Andhra Pradesh; yet, he and his supporters dreamt of it becoming the Yenan — the Red stronghold from where the Chinese revolution spread all over the country — of India. If wishes were horses, the communists would have made an excellent cavalry.

In August 1948, Ranadive exhorted the partymen to organize a mass-scale peasant uprising. There were to be general strikes, "the raiding of the police stations, zamindar and jotedar houses; ambushing police parties. . . sabotaging enemy communication lines, cutting of telephone and telegraph lines. . . . " Everything was to be done with the thoroughness associated with the military; there should be a single chain of command; there shouldn't be any doubts, misgivings, or pangs of conscience; it was underground Stalinism, as the party was declared illegal in several parts of the country and was generally facing repression. Without even coming to power, the communist leadership tried to launch purges! It was Joshi's good luck that he survived liquidation.

Ranadive started losing popularity in the party mainly because in the middle of 1948 thousands of miles away realization dawned upon the Soviet theoreticians that India was not at a stage to adopt violent means. This made the reservations of the moderates like Joshi, Dange, and Ajoy Ghosh creditable. Meanwhile Andhra communists also showed their disagreement with the Ranadive line that India must follow the Marxist doctrine and the Russian experience. They felt that the Maoist ideology and the Chinese experience were more relevant, and that the entire peasantry including the middle peasantry, could be won over for the cause of the revolution.

It was during this ideological confusion and political vicissitudes that a Cominform editorial, "A Lasting Peace for a People's Democracy", appeared in January 1950 which generally approved the Chinese form of struggle in Asian countries. It caused unprecedented confusion and hairsplitting in the party circles — akin to the theological debates in medieval Europe on the subjects like "How many angels can dance on the head of a needle?" In the editorial, it was said that "the party should align with all the peasantry." Raj Thapar, who along with her husband Romesh Thapar was closely associated with the party leadership, has given a vivid account of the havoc wrought by this simple sentence. She writes in *All These Years*:

> This rather sleepy sentence had sent shock waves among the theorizers, for after all the Soviets were omniscient and this editorial must surely have been written by RPD (Rajni Palme Dutt), as it was. So, who knows better? Certainly, not the comrades working at the grassroots!
>
> Ajoy Ghosh was in the process of formulating a more acceptable line than Ranadive's, but was so shaken by those few words that his thinking had come to a grinding halt. Day after day, he would ring our doorbell at ten in the morning, settle down with Romesh and start, Romesh, what do you think they mean by all the peasantry? It well near drove me mad with rage. The leader of the revolution, looking like an emaciated owl with his high receding forehead and his funny ears, intoning those words in his modulated voice as a kind of regular punctuation mark, for me it was the mantra of disillusion in a way. . . .
>
> I was beginning to react unfavorably to what I considered was the abysmal incapacity of communist "leaders". I kept questioning this business of receiving orders, formulations from abroad, while those who were supposedly in the "vanguard of the working class" had no say in the matter.

As a way out of the quandary, Ghosh "struck on what he considered a brilliant idea. He turned to me and said, 'Why don't you go to London and get us a confirmation from RPD?' I was caught off guard and bewildered, and protested."

Yet, she was persuaded by her husband and "the leader of the revolution" to go to London.

> When I told him [RPD] I. . . had come [to London] on a very important mission he sounded quite worried. I went on, "Ajoy wants to know whether 'all the peasantry' means all the peasantry." There was a moment's incredulous silence on the other end. I further explained that I was referring to the Cominform article, "Oh", he said. "Naturally, all the peasantry means all the peasantry! What else it could mean, my dear." Yes, what else it could have possibly meant? How right he was.

Leftist writers may lambaste Raj Thapar's indignation at the spinelessness and robotism of the communist leadership as the frustration of a renegade; for, she and her husband were some of the most important Left-of-the-Centre intellectuals who were later disillusioned by the communists. But the fact remains that in October 1950 Ajoy Ghosh's speech was quoted in a party journal in which he said that "nobody in the Indian Party can solve this problem. . . . Only [our international comrades] can help us. We must, therefore, contact the international leaders. None of us is clear what the Lasting Peace editorial means." Clarity and insight has to be imported. The Macaulayan in the communist would never trust the native wisdom or local experience; enlightenment has to come from the West, from "international comrades" who were influenced by a variety of factors.

An important factor was the onset of the Cold War between the US and the Soviet bloc, and this rendered the all-the-peasantry debate irrelevant. Moscow discovered in Nehru a useful sympathizer if not an ally; so, it promoted the idea that he was not "a running dog of imperialism", that he was essentially progressive but was pitted against the "Rightist elements" within the Congress, and that he should be supported by the communists. Such a line strengthened the moderate section represented by Ghosh, Dange, and PC Joshi.

As a consequence, the CPI started becoming pro-Congress. The main reason, of course, was the change of mood in Moscow. There were two indigenous factors as well: socialism and the foreign policy of Nehru. The pro-Congress tilt, however, was neither overnight nor total. According to the 1951 election manifesto of the CPI, "Five years of Congress rule — four of them after the attainment of 'freedom' — have brought our country and our people on the verge of disaster." Notice "freedom". It further thundered that Congress leaders "have betrayed our freedom struggle." Later, after the first elections were held in 1952, the party maintained that "disillusionment with the Congress was universal. Hatred against the Congress was mounting. . . . " In 1955, Ghosh wrote an article in the party mouthpiece, *The New Age*, titled "Nehru's Socialism — A Hoax." Yet, in spite of occasional outbursts, generally the CPI remained favorably inclined towards Nehru. For one, the communists have the remarkable quality of practicing and denouncing the same thing at the same time — and they can justify even that! They support liberalization and globalization in West Bengal, but not if it is done under the auspices of P Chidambaram whose government they support; they collaborate with the British during the Quit India movement, and have the temerity and brazenness to tell the Congress a couple of years later that they were supporting the freedom fighters. All in the name of ideology.

So, the pro-Nehru tilt was unmistakable. The Palghat Congress' political resolution of 1956 said that the CPI "will seek to mobilize all the democratic and progressive forces in all the parties, including Congress, for the immediate acceptance by the government of India, and for the rapid implementation by the various state governments, of the proposals made by the land reforms panel of the Planning Commission." Further, "although the Congress is the political party of the bourgeoisie which has taken many landlords in its fold, it has among its members a vast number of democratic elements. It has an anti-imperialist and democratic tradition. . . ."

The CPI's support to the Congress in the fifties was almost invariably accompanied by "although", "but", etc; nonetheless, it was support — ideological, intellectual, political, if not electoral. In its fascination for Nehru and other "progressive elements" in the Congress, and its detestation of "Right reactionaries", the CPI leadership adopted an ostrich-like attitude: it refused to recognize the fact that most of the "progressive elements" were no different from the non-progressive elements as far as political morality and adherence to scruples were concerned; some of the "progressives" were actually racketeers like VK Krishna Menon. They had crammed all the fashionable slogans of the time; by posturing as radicals, they were promoting their own prospects.

As government control over the economy increased, more opportunities opened up for self-seekers, hangers-on, and courtiers. Such characters merged with the Left-of-the-Centre elements, influencing and learning from each other. It was a soothing hallucination: life became comfortable for many progressive elements, and that too fully justified by ideology! It was a nice way of doing a revolution.

Not all in the CPI were, however, convinced that revolution would come by collaborating with the Establishment or allying with the Congress. This radical section had better appreciation of the ground realities. It clearly saw that Nehru's socialism was a grand farce, that the rich were becoming richer and the poor poorer, that his liberalism and democracy were also hypocritical, as demonstrated by the dismissal of the EMS Namboodiripad government in Kerala in 1959.

Not surprisingly, the differences within the CPI before the formal split in 1964 were mainly pertaining to the attitude towards and relations with the Congress. The communist leadership was mostly moderate, generally favorably disposed towards the Congress under Nehru. They were supported and encouraged by the Soviet Union which was increasingly finding Nehru to be a useful pawn in the chessboard of superpower politics. The reaction of the Indian government to the Soviet aggression in Hungary in 1956 proved this point. While the CPI leadership supported Nehru on almost all important issues, the radicals did the opposite; India's China policy was not an exception. Dange supported Nehru and, therefore, India; leaders like Jyoti Basu were pro-China (Sitaram Yechury still doesn't condemn the treachery and aggression of China).

Over the years, this tendency to ally with a stronger party developed into the full-fledged political method of bandwagonism. The CPI's flirtation with the Congress for a long period culminated in political marriage in 1969. This, however, ended in a divorce when the Congress was defeated in 1977. After some time, the CPI found solace in the arms of its own breakaway group, the Communist Party of India (Marxist), which had become much stronger. Since then, it has faithfully toed the CPM line, as faithfully as once it was toeing the Congress line.

Domineering CPM

Why is it that the Communist Party of India (Marxist), CPM, always sets the agenda for the group it is part of? Whether it is the Left Front in West Bengal or the United Front at the Centre, CPM leaders exert an influence much disproportionate to their political strength? This often makes them overbearing. Two instances from the recent past will drive home the point. When HD Deve Gowda was prime minister, he met Shiv Sena chief Bal Thackeray. CPM general secretary Harkishan Singh Surjeet objected to this. In other words, to meet a public figure the prime minister of the largest democracy was supposed to seek the sanction of a party which had less than 10 per cent members in Parliament. Never before had so few people exercised so great an authority. Similarly, when the results of the 1998 general elections were out, and it was clear that the BJP and its allies had emerged as the largest group in the Lok Sabha, though still short of absolute majority, Surjeet pompously declared that the United Front would support the Congress to form the government to check the march of "communal forces." This without consulting, or even informing, the other UF constituents. He just assumed their acquiescence; they had to toe his line. That the later events came as a jolt for him is another story.

We have discussed the bandwagonism of the CPI, as also the dissenting group within it. This group was ill-at-ease with the CPI leadership's pro-Congress — or, to be more precise, pro-Nehru — tilt in the fifties and sixties. PC Joshi and other CPI senior leaders said in a note at the Fourth Congress at Palghat in 1956: "In our opinion the slogan of a national democratic coalition government will in the present circumstances most effectively enable the party to defeat and isolate the pro-imperialist and pro-feudal elements, forge an alliance with the national bourgeois elements and help realize the hegemony of the proletariat over the nationalist movement." There were many twists and turns in the CPI line, but, in general, the leadership adopted a sympathetic attitude towards the 'progressive' elements within the Congress headed by Nehru. The dissenters, however, remained skeptical of the progressive Congress elements as also of the ruling party's policies. It was on the Indo-Chinese border dispute that the differences within the CPI became serious. In October 1962, the CPI Secretariat issued a statement: "Reports of the government of India show that the Chinese forces have crossed to the south of the McMahon Line and thus violated Indian territory, though the Chinese deny this. The Communist Party of India has always maintained that the McMahon Line is the border of India. Hence all necessary steps to defend it are justified." This statement was resented by the radicals who felt that China was not the aggressor because a socialist country could not commit aggression. After myriad vicissitudes, the party formally split in 1964.

In 1964, the picture was quite clear: the CPI was close to the Soviet Union, and remained so for decades; the CPM got close to China. But the CPM's honeymoon with Beijing was short-lived. Sankar Ghosh writes in *Political Ideas and Movements in India*, "Later, particularly since the Naxalbari movement in Bengal in 1967, the Chinese communists charged that the CPI(M) has become a revisionist party while the CPI(M), in its turn, denounced what it described as the dogmatism and left-sectarianism of the Chinese communists." It was not unnatural, for Beijing had found more pliable tools and obedient pupils in the Naxalites. The Naxalite leader, Charu Majumdar, had made his allegiance to Mao unambiguous by his statement, "China's chairman is our chairman." As the CPI had found its fatherland in Russia in the People's War era in the early forties, the Naxalites found one in China.

This meant that the CPM had to fend for itself; it became free in spite of itself; now it had to charter its own course, without any "friendly" advice from the capitals of communist states. Being averse to toeing the line of anybody in the country, it decided to adopt an aggressive strategy: from now on, it would play a dominant role in any formation or movement it were to join. Better to dominate in a region than to be lackeys of the rulers at the Centre — this became the mantra for the CPM. EMS Namboodiripad, former general secretary of the CPM, told an interviewer in *The Pioneer* (14 June 1997): "Unless we are in a position to influence the shaping of policy, we shall not join a Government. This shows that unlike other parties we are not hankering after ministerial offices." This was the reason the CPM declined to join the United Front government in 1996, though the "hankering" remained: Jyoti Basu called the decision not to form the government — he was offered the prime minister's office — a "historic blunder."

The CPM strategy complemented perfectly with the bandwagonism of the CPI; the former loves to play Big Brother; the latter likes following the Big Brother, whether it is the Congress or the CPM.

The CPM's consistent anti-Congress line — the first deviation appeared in 1998 — made it popular in certain areas. Public memory being notoriously short, its traitorous stand on the Indo-Chinese border dispute and response to the 1962 war was forgotten. Over the years, it became the main communist party, especially in West Bengal. And this seems to be full of irony. For, the CPM was born as an internationalist party; it had differed from the parent CPI which believed that China was the aggressor. But, after some time, the CPM started behaving like a regional party: it was a transition from internationalism to regionalism bypassing the stage of nationalism. The fact that the CPM is little more than a regional party has not gone unnoticed, but it has not been properly explained.

Bengal has a long history of anti-Delhi feelings. Muslim rule began in India after the Battle of Tarain in 1192. It was Bakhtiyar Khalji who won Bengal for the Delhi-based Saltanat. He was appointed governor of Bengal, but his status was as good as that of an independent ruler. For a few years of Balban's rule (1246-84), it was brought under Delhi's control. It was, however, only during the Mughal period that Bengal became a proper province. After the decline of the Great Mughals, the nawabs functioned without much interference from Delhi. When the British ended the rule of nawabs, it was the Bengalis who first came into contact with the West. Not surprisingly, the province produced a number of remarkable men in the nineteenth and twentieth centuries: they were the first reformers, modern thinkers, and nationalist leaders. Gokhale was so impressed by the thinking and achievements of eminent Bengalis that he called it the Hellas of India: what Bengal thinks today, India thinks tomorrow. Not surprisingly, regional pride among Bengalis is remarkable. A comparison with Punjab will underline this. Both provinces were divided during Partition. But while the Punjabi language and culture are cherished mainly by Sikhs — Punjabi Hindus claim their mother tongue to be Hindi and Punjabi Muslims, Urdu — the Bengali language still unites Hindu and Muslim Bengalis. In fact, Bengali regionalism was the root cause of the bifurcation of Pakistan in 1971. Not surprisingly, people of West Bengal do not appreciate their leaders being the puppets of the Centre.

The CPM under Jyoti Basu exploited the anti-Delhi feelings of Bengalis and egged on their provincialism. It was in the fitness of things that the Left Front leaders of Bengal severely censured Khushwant Singh because he had called Rabindranath Tagore a bad translator. In the eighties, Basu fought tooth and nail against the Centre on the issue of the Bakreswar power plant; he was seen as the foremost champion of the interests of Bengal.

It is widely believed that the CPM's pro-peasant policies and programs has helped it rule West Bengal for so long. VK Ramachandran wrote about the CPM's achievements in rural areas in *Frontline* (11 July 1997):

> There have been two major sets of institutional changes in the countryside since the Left Front came to power. The first comes under the broad rubric of land reform.
>
> First, the Government, supported by political organizations of rural working people, implemented Operation Barga, a mass movement of tenant-cultivators supported by new land reform legislation and new forms of administrative action. Under Operation Barga, which began in 1978, the names of 14 million sharecroppers were written in the land records (Operation Barga involved important administrative and legal innovations as well).

The major consequences of Operation Barga were to ensure security of tenure for tenant-cultivators, to prevent their eviction by absentee or non-cultivating owners and to create new rights for registered tenants (in respect, for instance, of the amount of rent they paid and their entitlements to formal-sector credit and inputs in kind).

Secondly, about 1,262,000 acres of land held by individuals and households above the land-ceiling (ceiling-surplus land) have been acquired. There has been much litigation regarding this land, but by January 1991, about 912,000 acres were distributed to about two million households. Twenty-one per cent of all ceiling-surplus land distributed in India was distributed in West Bengal (West Bengal has less than 4 per cent of the total cultivable land in the country).

Other features of land reform include: the distribution of currently non-agricultural land vested in the state for purposes of afforestation, for agricultural use and for different forms of community use, and the distribution of small plots (not larger than 0.08 acre) of house-site to 250,000 agri labor, artisans and fishing-worker households. Another area of evident success is the social forestry programme.

The other major institutional change is associated with the establishment of a three-tier panchayat system. West Bengal was the first state of the country with a democratic three-tier panchayat system, with elections held every five years, and it has been the first state to establish a system of democratic planning and development administration. The parties of the Left Front, and among them the CPI(M), dominate the panchayat system as they do the legislature. . . .

Agricultural production, which had remained stagnant for about two decades, accelerated sharply in the 1980s. . . The rate of growth of agricultural production in West Bengal, which was substantially lower than the Indian average between 1965 and 1980, was the highest among the 17 most populous states in India in the 1980s and until 1991-92. . . .

There is no denying the fact that the countryside has stood firmly behind the Left Front for more than two decades. It did not waver even in 1984 when the Congress got an unprecedented mandate in the rest of India. In the panchayat elections of 1993, out of the 60,011 gram panchayat seats, the Left Front won 39,232, the CPM alone bagging 35,328 and the Congress, 16,300. On the other hand, in the Calcutta municipal elections, the LF got 45.62 per cent votes against 45.25 per cent of Congress.

That the CPM's success in West Bengal is mainly due to its pro-peasant policies and programmes is a truism. This also shows that had the communists taken the peasant cause all over the country in all earnestness right from the beginning, and not over-emphasized the importance of the proletariat, they would have been in a much better position than they are today.

The same LF, which is well-entrenched in West Bengal now, had effected the deindustrialization process in the late sixties in the name of radicalizing the working class. For, the communist-dominated United Front ministries in 1967 had engaged in reckless adventurism. The Labor Minister, Subodh Banerjee, had once said: "As long as we are in government, the police will not help employers during any agitation by employees." Those were the days when the trade union leader ruled the roost. It was in this period that the word "gherao" became part of common parlance, followed by the closure of many units and the flight of capital. Lipton, Brooke Bond, the Thapars, and Reckitt & Coleman were among the major groups which shifted base to Delhi. From 1981 to 1991, West Bengal's share of Central investments came down from 8.6 per cent to 7.1 per cent. Of course, the Congress government's antipathy towards Calcutta played some role in it, but the LF can't be absolved of its responsibility.

Times have changed. The CPM government is ardently wooing investments, Indian as well as foreign. Somnath Chatterjee, chairman, West Bengal Industrial Development Corporation, told a correspondent of *Business World* (22 June 1997), "There is no option but to depend on foreign money."

The CPM's trade union wing, the Centre for Indian Trade Unions (CITU), has undergone a metamorphosis. The *Business World* correspondent reported in the same issue that the CITU activists, "armed with portable public address systems, were actually preaching discipline and streetside manners." A far cry from the feverish anti-Establishment rhetoric of the sixties and seventies.

But industrial reconstruction in West Bengal has been painfully slow. Between 1991 and 1996, the state received 1,406 industrial approvals entailing investments worth Rs 31,526 crore. But only 30 projects, worth little more than Rs 1,900 crore, are "under construction."

Outlook, a news magazine, carried an opinion poll in its issue of 25 June 1997. According to the poll, 64 per cent of the people believed that the condition of people in the state had improved under Basu. But the magazine also reported that not a single primary school had been set up in the last 10 years and the state accounted for 70 per cent of the country's provident fund defaults.

We believe that one of the most important factors responsible for the LF's long rule in West Bengal was the bad track record of the Congress Party when Siddharth Shankar Ray was the chief minister. In the early seventies, a reign of terror was unleashed by the authorities to check the growth of Naxalism. Countless young men were murdered in fake encounters. Congress leaders in Bengal were seen as the henchmen of Delhi whose hands were red with the blood of the young. The party was seen as anti-Bengali; the CPM propaganda only made this impression look more authentic. Besides, Bengal Congress was hopelessly divided.

A good thing about communist rule in West Bengal — which has gone almost unnoticed even by Leftist intellectuals — is that the LF has kept the state quarantined against the virus of caste politics. This despite the fact that neighboring Bihar is the worst Mandal-infested region in the country. West Bengal is perhaps the only state where caste does not find much mention in the discussions on electoral arithmetic.

So far, so good. Till the general elections of 1998, the CPM was quite successful in goading and coercing its allies to toe its line, whether it was the ideologically kindred souls of the Left Front or the opportunist elements of the absurdly named United Front. The CPM's bullying boomeranged when Surjeet unilaterally announced the course of action the UF was supposed to take in the event of the BJP and its allies emerging as the largest group just short of majority. All of us would support the Congress to check the march of "communal forces," Surjeet announced pompously. Such unilateralism and pomposity proved to be the undoing of the CPM; this led to the vertical split in the UF, with front convenor and Andhra Pradesh Chief Minister Chandrababu Naidu doing a political somersault and supporting the BJP.

Further, in these times of ideological confusion and political promiscuity, the CPM can't take the support of its junior allies like the Revolutionary Socialist Party (RSP) and the Forward Block (FB) for granted, as now they have the option of allying with the BJP. In fact, they did oppose the CPM stand of support to the Congress, a stand which was a consequence of the CPM's rabid anti-BJP stand. If Leftists like George Fernandes and Nitish Kumar can become allies of the Right-wing BJP, a future BJP-RSP-FB alliance can't be ruled out. With Mamata Banerjee emerging as the foremost anti-Left leader in the state, and the presence of the Bharatiya Janata Party becoming more visible, the communist bastion may not remain as impregnable as it used to be earlier.

Summary

There are three interesting observations on the history of Indian communism. First, more often than not the success of a communist leader is directly proportional to his rootlessness. The Satyabhatkta-versus-MN Roy controversy is a paradigm case. At least in the communist hierarchy, class theory holds good: the suave, urbane, English-speaking people from affluent families dominate the communist parties, and they have supreme disdain for anything that is Hindu, ancient Indian, or traditional. The rank and file comprises activists from humbler origins whose idealism and fortitude has kept the cause of communism alive for so long. It was the faceless cadre who bore the brunt of state repression, kept the party machinery functional with their meager resources, and zealously campaigned for party candidates in elections; in New Delhi, the leader and the highbrow communist intellectual would just condemn the killing of the cadre in a remote area.

Second, the story of Indian communism is also the story of assimilation: gradually, grudgingly, most communist groups, including those of the extremist Naxalites, have accepted electoral politics.

Third, relations with the Congress have greatly influenced the course of communist history in India. As communist parties have become more assimilated within the Indian parliamentary system, their relations with the Congress have improved over the decades. For the first time in 1998, even the CPM, one of the most anti-Congress parties in the country.

CHAPTER 4

The Socialist Stream
or
The Pink Edge

Chemistry of Indian Socialism

It is not very often that a communist considers the contribution of any thinker greater than that of Karl Marx. Therefore, AB Bardhan's statement that BR Ambedkar was more relevant than Marx in the context of Dalit emancipation is significant. The general secretary of the Communist Party of India (CPI) admitted this at a seminar in Lucknow on 16 February 1997. In a way, Bardhan accepted that caste prevails over class at least in certain cases.

Such candor would have been blasphemous even ten years earlier. But then the world had undergone a metamorphosis in these ten years, the biggest change being the demise of the Soviet Union. China, too, galloped furiously towards the market economy. Not surprisingly, Indian communists suddenly felt lonely, if not orphaned. As no model existed outside the country, they, willy-nilly, had to come to terms with the realities of Indian politics.

Concomitantly, the stars of Vishwanath Pratap Singh were in the ascendance and, fortunately, he was favorably inclined towards communists. In fact, just after his estrangement with

Rajiv Gandhi, he had proclaimed that the Left was his "natural ally."

Singh is famous or infamous for his decision to implement the Mandal Commission report. However, another of his contributions — which is equally, if not more, important — has gone unnoticed: he brought communists and socialists together. But what is so great about bringing two ideologically kindred groups together? To find the answer, we have to see the genesis and growth of Indian socialism.

It was born with the Congress Socialist Party (CSP), a group of Leftists who formed a forum within the Congress. It included Acharya Narendra Deva, Jaiprakash Narayan, Achyut Patwardhan, Ashok Mehta, MR Masani, NG Goray, and SM Joshi.

Presiding over the first session of the All India Socialist Conference at Patna in May 1934, Acharya Narendra Dev emphasized the need to "broaden the basis" of the freedom movement "which has so far been a predominantly middle class movement."

Indian socialism is an eclectic ideology, a queer mixture of the beatific and the bizarre, of altruism and opportunism, of idealism and pragmatism, of liberalism and communism, and, above all, of Gandhi and Marx. It would not be an exaggeration to say that the history of Indian socialism is the history of audacious, even quixotic, attempts to reconcile the above-mentioned irreconcilables. The most daring and reckless have been the efforts to reconcile Gandhi with Marx. Perhaps, the socialists were condemned to endeavor this reconciliation; for, the influences of Gandhi as well as Marx were tremendous at that time. The Bolshevik Revolution had inspired many; the Soviet economy was booming at a time when the West was reeling under the worst depression. Besides, Soviet egalitarianism also increased the fascination for Marx. Simultaneously, the Indian socialists also came under the spell of Gandhi. Even those socialists who differed with Gandhi on crucial matters, like Jawaharlal Nehru, were greatly impressed by his simplicity and his ability to inspire the masses.

In other words, Marxism and Gandhism were the two essential ingredients of Indian socialism — though in its different brands they were present in different proportions. For instance, on Narendra Deva, the Marxian influence was more pronounced; on Jaiprakash Narayan, the Gandhian one. To these ingredients, other elements were also added. If it was the element of liberalism, the result was Nehru; if it was caste politics, it was Lohia and the Mandalites.

Another intended reconciliation has been between democracy and communism. Indian socialists, born and brought up in the (generally) British-liberal milieu, instinctively disliked a system in which all dissent is suppressed, the individual becomes powerless *vis-à-vis* the State, and freedom of expression is done away with; hence their predilection for democracy. Interestingly, Lohia was aware of this fact. He said, "Socialism should cease to live on borrowed breath. Too long it has borrowed from communism its economic aims and from capitalism or the liberal age its non-economic or general aims." But the incorrigible socialists, not excluding Lohia, continued to yearn for the economy of communism and the polity, or "general aims", of democracy; they wanted the best of both worlds. Nehru also wanted the egalitarianism of communism and the liberalism of democracy. It is another matter that what we got in the bargain was the worst of both worlds — viz., the inequalities of "bourgeois" democracy and the bureaucratized economy of communism.

Nehru, though never a member of the CSP, was favorably disposed towards the Congress Socialists. When he became president of the Indian National Congress in 1936, he appointed Jaiprakash Narayan, Narendra Deva, and Achyut Patwardhan to the Congress Working Committee. Within the Congress, the socialists functioned as a pressure group, trying to put radical programs on the political agenda. Fed up with their over-zealousness, Sardar Vallabbhai Patel decided to discipline them in 1948. They were asked to disband their outfit or quit the

Congress; they chose the latter alternative. Writes Sankar Ghosh in his *Political Ideas and Movements in India*:

> In May 1951, Acharya Kripalani formed the Kisan Mazdoor Praja Party (KMPP), mainly from the persons who had seceded from the Congress. Later, after the 1952 elections, in August 1952 the KMPP and the Socialist Party merged. The new party formed as a result of such merger was called the Praja Socialist Party (PSP)....
>
> In February 1953 there were certain talks, which eventually proved unsuccessful, about the prospects of co-operation between the Congress and the PSP both within and outside the government. This plea of co-operation between the PSP and the Congress was opposed by Acharya Narendra Deva and particularly by Ram Manohar Lohia. ...
>
> Soon thereafter a further crisis developed within the PSP. In Travancore-Cochin, where the ministry was headed by the PSP Chief Minister, Pattom Thanu Pillai, police had to fire on certain demonstrators. Deploring the firing taken place under a socialist government, Dr. Lohia, the general secretary of the PSP, sent a cable to the chief minister asking him to resign after instituting a judicial inquiry into the firing. The chief minister refused to do so. So, Dr. Lohia resigned from the general-secretaryship of the party. Though the National Executive and a special convention of the party supported the chief minister, there was a sharp division in the party over the question of firing. ...
>
> Further difficulties were in store for the party. After the Congress at its Avadi session in 1955 declared its faith in a socialistic pattern of society, the Bombay group of the party issued a statement that the party's policy of non-cooperation with the Congress had become obsolete. Madhu Limaye, who was close to Lohia. .., charged that Ashok Mehta had inspired this statement. The then party chairman, Acharya Narendra Deva, asked Limaye to withdraw the charge. Instead of withdrawing the charge, Limaye repeated it. Limaye was then suspended by the executive of the Bombay city PSP. Dr. Lohia was also suspended.
>
> Dr. Lohia left the PSP and sought to revive the old Socialist Party. This weakened the PSP, and the party was further weakened when JP Narayan declared that he would leave politics

and join the bhoodan and sarvodaya movement. The death of Acharya Narendra Deva, in 1957, was another blow for the party.

The PSP fared badly in the 1957 general elections. Thereafter attempts were made to bring about a rapprochement between the PSP and Dr. Lohia and his party, but without success.

In the 1962 elections both the PSP and the Socialist Party fared badly. . .

Later, in March 1964, Dr. Lohia spoke in favor of the merger of the Socialist Party with the PSP, and as a result of the merger which took place in June 1964 the Samyukta Socialist Party (SSP) was formed. But, in spite of the merger. . . .

Loitering for years futility on the political landscape made the socialists not only frustrated but also politically promiscuous. Slowly but steadily, the emphasis shifted from ideology to strategy. And Lohia emerged as the chief strategist. It was the Lohiaite strategy of anti-Congressism which deposed the seemingly invincible Congress regime in 1977 and again in 1989.

Not that all socialists were always anti-Congress; there were many who thought that blind anti-Congressism was useless and opportunistic (how else an alliance with the Bharatiya Jana Sangh, the precursor of the BJP, could be understood, they asked). In fact, relations with the Congress have always generated controversies, debates, and bickering among the socialists as well as communists. Among the latter, there has been no dearth of people like SA Dange who considered Nehru as progressive and support to whom, it was argued, would further the cause of the downtrodden. And there was socialist Ashok Mehta who actually joined the Union cabinet after being dismissed from the PSP. However, the line which was generally accepted by the seventies was that of Lohia: oppose the Congress at any cost. Even Jaiprakash Narian followed it. The result was 1977.

The logic prevailed for the last time in 1989 under VP Singh. The novelty in his contribution was that he made the communists and the Janata Dal (which was dominated by socialists) not only strategic allies but also political friends. And this honeymoon outlived his regime. Never before had the ties between the two streams of the Indian Left been stronger. Only once had they come as close, but that was more a result of the diktats of the Comintern than of the genuine desire to work with each other. The rise of fascism in Europe in the twenties and thirties had alarmed Moscow. The Comintern thought that an alliance with socialists all over the world would help check the tide of fascism. Enunciating the Comintern line, Rajni Palme Dutt and Ben Bradley, members of the Communist Party of Great Britain, published an article "The Anti-imperialist People's Front in India" in February 1936. According to what came to be known as the Dutt-Bradley thesis, "Congress Socialists, trade unionists, communists, and Left Congressmen should all unite on the essentials of a minimum programme of anti-imperialist struggle for complete independence."

Though the CSP welcomed the new communist line as "remarkable", there were some socialists who had their doubts and apprehensions. Ashok Mehta wrote, "Anti-imperialist front must not be for building dictatorship of the Communist Party. . . . Co-operation today and concentration camp tomorrow is an unfortunate tactic." Senior leaders Narayan and Narendra Deva, however, were quite favorably inclined towards the communists. During 1936-39, there was close co-operation between the socialists and communists. According to Madhu Limaye, "The communist elements within the CSP kept intact their links with the underground CPI, obeyed its orders, gave no loyalty to the CSP principles and resolution, did faction work and tried to win over the confused and non-committed elements of the CSP."

About half a century later, however, it was Mikhail Gorbachev who was calling the shots in Moscow, and he was too busy setting his own house in order to bother about the chances of revolution in India. As a cruel joke on Marx, he in fact played the key role in the withering away of the first socialist state of the world. Therefore, Indian communists did not have any difficulties in forging an alliance with the VP Singh group.

But can VP Singh be called a socialist? In politics, says Will Durant, the longest distance between two points is the straight line; nowhere is it more appropriate than in Indian politics. It is amazing but true that the member of a former royal family redefined the neo-Left in India. For, he had the perspicacity to understand the subterranean currents of Indian politics. Singh understood the political sociology of the eighties better than most of the leaders did. He recognized the political aspirations of the middle peasantry, most of them being of backward castes. These castes had improved their lot to some extent by the eighties; and, being numerically significant, they were becoming more assertive in the political arena. Singh capitalized on the political ambitions of these castes.

Most analysts and commentators feel that the announcement of the implementation of the Mandal Commission recommendations in August 1990 was a hasty move, a move to clip the wings of Chaudhary Devi Lal. Devi Lal might have been the immediate cause, but Singh had already made up his mind in favor of Mandalization. The August 1990 announcement set the new agenda and redefined the neo-Left: the poor and the exploited became synonymous with backwards and dalits; the rich and the elite, with the forwards castes.

It is a paradox that while Singh bestowed respectability and relevance on the caste-based ideology of Lohia, he also delivered a mortal blow to the Lohiaite strategy of anti-Congressism. For, the acceptance of Mandal's report crucified Lohia the strategist and rejuvenated Lohia the ideologue. Singh could have said, "Lohia is dead, long live Lohia!"

There were two consequences of the intense anti-Mandal agitation. First, this came to be seen as an anti-reservation stir. Interestingly, this was made possible as much by the anti-Mandal activists as by the Mandalites. To begin with, the subtext of the Mandal report played a key role in blurring the distinctions between the non-upper castes. Reservation for the backwards was justified as they had been exploited and oppressed by the upper castes. But all evidence, historical as well as mythological, given in the report pertains to the exploitation of and discrimination against the *shudras*, or dalits, and *not* the backward castes. Now, the dalits had already been enjoying the benefit of reservation; so, how could the backwards claim to be compensated for the ill-treatment suffered by the dalits? The Mandal Commission report confronts this dilemma by presenting a tragic narrative in which the non-upper castes are a monolithic mass of suffering humanity, the brahmins are scheming patriarchs, other upper castes are willing collaborators of the Machiavellian priests, and caste is the instrument of oppression. "If religion was ever used as an opium of the masses, it was done in India, where a small priest-class, by a subtle process of conditioning the thinking of the vast majority of the people hypnotized them for ages into accepting a role of servility and humility," says the Mandal Commission report. Further, "As laborers, cultivators, craftsmen, etc, *shudras* were the main producers of social surplus. . . they had no right to private property; they carried the main burden of taxes, and the heaviest punishments were awarded to them for minor infringements of the social code. As their low caste status was tied to their birth, they toiled and suffered without hope."

This is an excellent melange of the true and the untrue, of fact and fiction, of history and mythology; but it did strike a sympathetic chord in the hearts of many backwards and dalits. Here was an ideology they could embrace. Its *modus operandi*, reservations, would redeem them. Or so they thought.

The reaction of upper castes, too, helped blur the distinctions between the backwards and dalits, as they did not conceal their antipathy to the very concept of reservation; the dalits also found the agitation to be potentially dangerous to their interests.

It was VP Singh who set the agenda for the nineties. To counter Mandal, the BJP was goaded to adopt an aggressive stance. This aggression continued in the demolition of the Babri Masjid on 6 December 1992. The increasing bellicosity and strength of the BJP brought the socialists and communists even closer. So much so that even the veteran communist leaders started noticing some merit in the caste-based ideologies of Ambedkar and Lohia.

Not that the communists have replaced the doctrine of caste struggle with that of caste war, but a long association of casteists is bound to have some repercussions.

Phony Revolutionary

VP Singh's fans maintain that he is a messiah who could have redeemed the teeming millions of the country had the villainish, upper caste, 'elitist,' oh-so-bad middle classes not precluded this. But the fact is that his ideology and strategy were fundamentally flawed. For, essentially there is no difference between the bureaucratic socialism of Jawaharlal Nehru and the Mandal-brand egalitarianism of Singh. Nehru felt that the state is capable of performing miracles in all spheres of life and that it can provide solutions to all the problems plaguing the country. So, the Indian state got involved in a host of activities; its role increased phenomenally in the economy, from running steel factories to hotels; the bureaucracy expanded and became stronger and ubiquitous. Thanks to the incompetence, unscrupulousness, and populism of the political class, bureaucrats' control over the economy became a stranglehold. Hence the myriad licenses, permits, quotas, and the permit-quota raj, and the inspector raj, and the raid raj, and the concomitant corruption. And hence the charm of civil services, where even professionally qualified people like doctors and engineers tried their luck.

Singh's bible, the Mandal Commission report, says, "In India, the state is by far the largest employer and the greatest dispenser of all sorts of patronage." (When the Supreme Court chided Satish Sharma for handling the Petroleum Ministry as his "feudal property," he replied that "this was standard practice." Unfortunately, he was not lying.) However, the Mandalites don't find anything immoral or anti-democratic in the state being "the greatest dispenser of all sorts of patronage," which essentially is a feudalistic hangover; there is nothing wrong about the discretionary quotas of the Satish Sharmas; what is wrong is the social background of the beneficiaries. The beneficiaries should be non-forward castes. A minister in the HD Deve Gowda government actually said that if the forward castes can exploit the country for thousands of years, why can't the backwards be allowed to do the same for 50 years. They don't want to change the iniquitous, feudalistic system; they just want their place in the sun.

Why is the state "the greatest dispenser of all sorts of patronage" in the *weltanschauungs* of Nehru and VP Singh? This is because basically there is little difference between the two; only in the nuances do they differ. A socio-psychological analysis of the class in ascendance in the 1940s and 1950s will help.

The intelligentsia, for all its love for Western ideas and ideals, remained brahmanical in one respect: it continued to disdain commerce and manual labor; even today, the scene has not changed radically. So, the job that was considered ideal for a young man was the one in which he did not have to soil his hands or clothes. Medicine and engineering became coveted professions. Another coveted vocation was government service. Its biggest plus point is the security of tenure: this security is a boon for those who prefer stability over progress; it is also a shield for the inefficient and the indolent.

The intelligentsia's brahmanical scorn for business blended magically with the socialistic disdain for private enterprise. The result was an ever-expanding government sector and a stunted private sector. In other words, productive work and productivity were ignored, and egalitarian, socialistic slogans replaced rational policy making. Gradually, all the grand objectives — to attain which public sector undertakings were set up — were relegated to oblivion and providing employment to more and more people became an end in itself; later, it became the sole motive. The economic resources at the disposal of ministers and officials increased over the years. And since pleasing friends and relatives has always been considered the done thing in India, dispensing "all sorts of patronage" has seldom been frowned upon.

Another brahmanical feature, we-are-superior-to-the-others syndrome, also became an integral part of the mindset of the ruling class. This class was becoming more and more susceptible to the socialistic beliefs and ideas. Again the superiority complex established a wonderful chemistry with Leftist doctrines. "We are divinely ordained to redeem the toiling masses" — the powers-that-be got intoxicated by this idea. Anybody who dared to challenge the validity of divine contract, or the *modus operandi* of the redemption, was branded as a "Right reactionary". Hence C Rajgopalachari, Minoo Masani, Deen Dayal Upadhyaya, and other prominent leaders were demonized and marginalized. Needless to say, the ruling class found willing allies in intellectuals who were mostly of Leftist orientation.

Philanthropy, said the famous British imperialist Cecil Rhodes, is good, but with 5 per cent profit it's a good deal made better. In India, too, philanthropy was found to be profitable. Socialism, in theory, means the nation's control over the economy. In practice, however, the "nation" means Jayalalitha and Sukh Ram; it also means the arrogant and corrupt bureaucrat, the unscrupulous middleman, the tout. As the most articulate sections of the intellectual class allied with the Establishment in the Great Philanthropic Project of setting up a "socialistic pattern of society", the honeymoon between the two went on unabated; scholars, academics, writers, economists, litterateurs, journalists provided reasons for establishing "a socialist state", which Jawaharlal Nehru wanted to do; corrupt practices that accompanied the project were glossed over (Nehru shielded Menon; Indira Gandhi called corruption a "global phenomenon"). All this for the sake of the Great Philanthropic Project of helping the poorest of the poor, the downtrodden, the wretched of the earth.

Thanks to the us/them dichotomy, it was never seriously considered that "they" — the poorest of the poor, the downtrodden — could also help themselves if the circumstances were conducive; that "they" were also blessed with the faculties of mind; that it was possible that "they" could themselves bring about their salvation; that "they" might be illiterate but not necessarily unintelligent; that "they" might be without resources but not without ingenuity, without food but not without honor. The basic premises of "us" were: "we" are enlightened because "we" know what is science and technology, and the wonders they are capable of performing; "we" know what is development; "we" know the telos of human existence; "we" know Voltaire and Rousseau, Milton and Mill, Marx and Darwin, rationalism and humanism. And "we" shall tell the subalterns about such things; "we" shall redeem "them."

Philanthropy turned out to be lucrative occupation. It would surprise nobody that because of such haughty altruism, some of the biggest frauds were committed in the name of helping the poor. Rajiv Gandhi almost confessed the failure of the Indian state in helping the downtrodden when he said in the mid-eighties that only 15 paise reached the targeted beneficiaries out of every rupee spent by the government. By liberalizing the economy, PV Narasimha Rao and Manmohan Singh gave up the plans, if not pretensions, to salvage the teeming millions.

VP Singh and other Mandalites have, however, not given up such plans and pretensions. VP Singh repeatedly claims, "*We* want to let *them* participate in the affairs of state." How? Of course, by reservations, caste-based reservations, and still more caste-based reservations. The project is, to put it mildly, quixotic. For, it is impossible for the government to provide jobs to the crores of unemployed people. There are limits beyond which even "the greatest dispenser of all sorts of patronage" can't go.

Mandalization of Indian Communism

Janata Dal leader Sharad Yadav's tirade against the *parkati mahila* (the woman with bobbed hair) in May 1997, during a debate in Parliament on the Women's Reservation Bill, sent shock waves throughout elitist Leftist circles. The term he used was indeed offensive; he realized his indiscretion and apologized for it. Yadav replaced the term with *bhadralok* women, but his line of argument remained the same: "there is a marked difference between our women and those from forward castes"; these "elite women" do not represent all women as they "do not understand the problems of women living in the villages and the slums."

This debate between communists, the most vociferous champions of the Bill, and Mandalite socialists could have been a watershed between the two streams of the Indian Left. The vehemence with which backward caste leaders like Yadav demanded quota for "their" women nonplused the English-speaking, suave, urban, and urbane Leftists. Their response was full of anger and anguish. However, serious cracks did not appear in the communist-socialist alliance.

But at a deeper, subtler level, a remarkable transformation was happening: the Mandalization of Indian communism. For the acceptance of gender as a basic category is, to put it mildly, a negation of the basic tenet of Marxism, namely the class theory; it is worse than the most pernicious revisionism ever attempted. If gender precedes class, then all that Marx has said becomes outdated. Not that communists were completely oblivious of this reality; they just pretended to be ignorant. Such was the sway of Mandalization. Malini Bhattacharya, a prominent leader of the Communist Party of India (Marxist) wrote in *Seminar* (September 1997):

> We know that women in legislative bodies, like men, represent political parties. The political ideology of the party and the class interests represented by the party are manifested in the performance of the members as a people's representative. . . . Women from the dominant parties, that is, parties representing the ruling class, will represent their ideological interests, and their percentage will be highest among the newly-elected women. Reservation cannot change this. Yet, it will also ensure the presence of some women with a commitment to the exploited classes.

Even if a small percentage of newly-elected women representatives raise their voice to highlight the needs, rights and demands of these classes, it will be a step towards the democratization of politics.

Bhattacharya is aware that women in "the dominant parties. . . will represent their ideological interests." So, how "the presence of some women" will have a "commitment to the exploited classes?" If it is the class interests which guide the actions of politicians, as per Marxian tenets, how would "women representatives raise their voice to highlight the needs, rights and demands of" the exploited? These questions can't be answered without taking the Mandalite assumptions into account. First, we will have to assume that women representatives themselves are a caste — a few politically correct intellectuals have actually said so. Second, we will have to accept Mandal's central thesis: emancipation is strictly an intra-group affair; it is only the empowered individuals who can help in the uplift of their less-privileged sisters in the group. It was in the early nineties, when reservation for OBCs was being discussed, that this line of argument was proffered by the champions of social justice. They claimed that an upper caste person in a high office is unable to empathize with the pathos of the downtrodden who are, according to Mandalites, all lower caste people. For upper caste people, the problems of the poor are an intellectual affair; for the lower caste empowered individuals, it would be an existential matter. According to this perverse "existentialist" philosophy, the upper castes can think about poverty; the rest have felt it. Hence   the Mandal Commission's report. And hence the Women's Reservation Bill.

Thanks to their disdain for empirical evidence, the communists never bothered to find out how many Musahars, who are among the poorest castes in the country, have benefited from the quota for Scheduled Castes, or how many Telis and Kumhars have been redeemed by Mandal. That reservations have only created a "creamy layer" among the dalits and OBCs is a well-known fact; the communists failed to recognize this simple fact. They kept on parroting the clicked slogans: legislative bodies are "exclusive men's clubs"; the representation of women in the Lok Sabha was just 7 per cent in 1996; women are "conspicuous by their absence" in political space; women have been "losing faith in the political process;" and so on. While the verbose feminist-Leftist accounts discussed the miserable plight of Indian women, the two main communist parties were without a single woman in their politburos!

Another fact that was glossed over was the prime-ministership of Indira Gandhi. She ruled the country for fifteen years, but her regime was no different from any other as far as the woman question was concerned; at least, there is no empirical evidence to suggest that her governance played any role in improving the lot of women. But then empirical evidence is something the communists disdain. They are dialectical materialists, not empiricists!

Tryst with Bureaucratic Socialism

In India, economic policy is not formulated after taking into account the ground realities; it is an echo of the fads in vogue in the West. So, when open economy became a rage everywhere — even China went for market socialism — the Indian economy was also liberalized, in a similar manner as once India had made a tryst with socialism under the first prime minister.

Jawaharlal Nehru, like many other Leftists, was attracted towards socialist ideas not because of their relevance in India but because they were fashionable in the intellectual circles of the West during the thirties and forties. While the Soviet Union was making giant strides in the economy, the capitalist world was reeling under a debilitating depression. Since the commitment to socialism did not come from the soil — as it did in, say, China and Cuba — socialism became a boon for politicians and bureaucrats. The objectives of Indian socialism were noble, but they could not be attained. It was not that Nehru was not sincere about his commitments, nor was it because of the diabolic designs of the "Right reactionaries" that the Great Philanthropic Project failed. The project was doomed from the beginning.

To begin with, the political system was not in tune with the project. There was, and is, democracy in India; this meant that the state could not use coercion limitlessly to implement economic policies. The Soviet Union, China, and other socialist countries never faced this dichotomy between the polity and the economy. In our country, socialistic measures were bound to be half-hearted.

Further, there was lack of human material. In the Soviet Union and China, there was a cadre committed to the ideals of socialism. It was not only the top leadership that captured office but also the rank and file that became an integral part of the new dispensation. The change was total. In India, however, the state apparatus remained the same in all respects but the name: the ICS became the IAS; the police and the military, too, did not change. One reason for this was Gandhism. Since Gandhi wanted to do away with the state *per se*, he, as leader of the Congress, did nothing to prepare the cadre for free India. The top brass of the Congress, too, got tired of fighting the British; Nehru admitted this fact later. The leaders had had enough of movements and jails; now, they wanted to enjoy themselves. They wanted the pleasure of being in office. Which they did for a long time — of course, at the expense of the country. This was in sharp contrast to what happened in, say, China. A communist leader told Edgar Snow, "First we fought the Japanese, then we chased out the Kuomintang. When we had won we laid down our rifles and immediately picked up tools." (*The Other Side of the River: Red China Today*).

In India, it was the bureaucrats who took charge of reconstruction, or whatever went in its name. Nehru proved to be their biggest benefactor, which is ironical because he was not said to be favorably disposed towards them, "the steel frame of the British Empire" as they were called.

It would be pertinent to examine the roots of Indian socialism *as it was practiced*, not as it was preached. The British did succeed to a large extent in creating a class of people Indian in blood and color, but Western in taste, opinion, morals, and intellect. But some residues remained; one of them was the brahmanical contempt for agriculture, industry, business, and trade; and this bias synergistically combined with the socialist ideas and ideals. Therefore, it might appear paradoxical but it is true that Indian socialism helped preserve one of the most pernicious features of brahmanism — scorn for any production-related activity.

It is a well-known fact of history that ebb in trade has always followed an overall decline in various spheres of life: the fragmentation of polity; rise in social rigidities like the ban on sea travel; more burden of land revenue on peasantry as feudal lords grow in number and the central authority weakens. The country becomes more and more isolated from the world. Not surprisingly, one of the most conspicuous signs of the decline of the glory of ancient India is the paucity of coins in the sixth and seventh centuries of the Christian era. On the other hand, revival of trade played a key role in ending the Dark Ages in Europe and ushering in the Renaissance and, later, the Enlightenment. When the British brought the Enlightenment to Indian shores — rationalism and humanism, Voltaire and Rousseau, Mill and Bentham — the Indian intelligentsia was born. It was, says Girilal Jain in *The Hindu Phenomenon*, Nehru's "constituency." These people "came from modest non-business, indeed anti-business, backgrounds, the priestly brahmin one being the most important. They could regard themselves as members of the middle class, largely on the strength of their educational qualifications and entitlement of white collar jobs. Their first search was for security of employment with the government which also happened to be the only truly big employer of educated Indians." Jain adds that "Nehru was their ideal from the time of his rise to prominence in the Indian National Congress, the party of the freedom movement, in the twenties."

Howsoever Westernized the intelligentsia might have become in its political outlook, it did not shed its inveterate contempt for business, agriculture, and industry. This was the class that dominated the freedom movement (It is to be noted that the nationalist movement started with the demand of the Indianization of services.) Not surprisingly, in the first few decades of Independence, the intelligentsia — despite being numerically insignificant — dominated the intellectual and public discourse. And its brahmanical anti-business bias got ideological justification in socialism. Such were the social roots of socialism.

When this anti-business class manned the government machinery, it played havoc with entrepreneurship. "Bureaucrats were not slow to take advantage of the unprecedented opportunity that had unexpectedly come their way," says Jain.

> They created a web of controls and regulations of Byzantine complexity, through which they alone could help desperate businessmen find their way, of course, for a fee. In course of time, India became one of the most regulated economies of the world, and thereby one of the most corrupt polities and bureaucracies.
>
> Socialism, a euphemism for an economy dominated by bureaucrats and politicians, was the central pillar of the Nehruvian system and that essentially remained the same under Indira Gandhi and Rajiv Gandhi.

The middle class disdain for productive labor still continues, and it has seeped into common parlance and social attitude. *Lala* is a derogatory term for any reasonably well-off businessman. Another term, *seth*, is often pejoratively used for the rich in Hindi films. In this context, a bizarre incident deserves mention. In the 1980s, Upendranath Ashk, a Hindi author of repute, opened a grocery shop in a UP town. This sent shock waves throughout the Hindi-speaking world. What a disgrace that a great writer has to run a shop to make both ends meet, said people. The indignation was widespread. Few, if any, had the temerity to question the basis of indignation. What was wrong with running a grocery shop? After all, it is not a dishonorable, immoral, or illegal profession. The fuss was about the fact that a "great" man had to do a "lowly" job!

At the heart of the failure of socialism lies Nehru's obsession for rhetoric on the one hand, and disdain for empirical evidence on the other. The romance was nationalization — the nation's control over the economy; the reality was that more often than not the nation meant Sukh Ram, Sheila Kaul, Laloo Prasad Yadav, and other such luminaries. Now, this sounds blasphemous. It may be pointed out that this is an unwarranted and malicious generalization, a scurrilous evaluation of the Nehruvian order, that the Sukh Rams and the Laloo Yadavs are exceptions rather than the rule, that it was not so earlier. In fact, Leftists point out that the scam-a-day scenario of today is actually a result of liberalization and the abandonment of socialism. But then the Leftist narrative resembles a grand theological saga in which liberalization is the original sin, the public sector is angelic, and the big, bad multinationals are diabolic.

Nehru's disdain for facts is best illustrated in the way he protected and promoted VK Krishna Menon; it can be seen as a paradigm case. Menon became the prime minister's favorite, so much so that he has been called Nehru's alter ego. Menon was stuck neck-deep in the jeep scandal in 1948. At that time, the country was at war with Pakistan over Kashmir; and the Army was short of 4,600 jeeps. Menon, as High Commissioner in London, placed an order worth over Rs 80 lakh to a company whose capital assets did not exceed £605! The company was to be paid 65 per cent of the money on the receipt of clearance certificates from the inspecting firm. But it was paid that amount within a month of signing the contract without inspection certificates. The payment was sarcastically explained by B Shiva Rao, a member of the Congress Parliamentary Party's Committee on the scandal, "because with its incredibly meager resources it (the company) would never have been in a position to fulfill that contract without the amount being advanced to it."

Menon was also involved in several other fraudulent deals, one of these being the purchase of rifles and ammunition. A £2 million contract was signed with a firm whose issued capital was £100. Since the culpability of Menon was too glaring to be glossed over, the Public Accounts Committee, in its Ninth Report, recommended that the deals be "assessed by a high-level committee, consisting of one or two High Court judges." The Nehru government — instead of punishing Menon — requested the Committee to "reconsider their earlier recommendations" (September 1953). When the Committee declined to do so, the case was closed in 1955. And the punishment Menon received? He became a minister in the Union cabinet in the following year! According to Surendranath Dwivedy and GS Bhargava, in their book *Political Corruption in India,* "What is known as the jeep scandal belongs to a class by itself. It was the first of its kind to come to light in free India. . . . An impression had been created that the corrupt could go away with it if they were on the right side of the rulers. The result was that more and more people took to public dishonesty almost as a policy, while mouthing radical slogans and striking a Leftist posture." Not surprisingly, Menon was a Leftist. In fact, a symbiotic relationship evolved between the Left and the Establishment (discussed in other chapters).

The inherent weaknesses of the Great Philanthropic Project became quite apparent after some time. As there was no dictatorship, public sector enterprises could not be forced to show results; work was done in accordance with the time-consuming bureaucratic procedures; the mindset was out of sync with industrial society ethos. There were political interference, official apathy, and aggressive unions. The politician and the bureaucrat, in any case, were interested in building properties, not socialism. On top of everything, there was the Menon legacy: one could keep milking the public exchequer, while making all the right noises about socialism, egalitarianism, and social justice; there would be no reprimand, rebuke, or retribution; in fact, one could even climb the socio-political ladder. For it was in the days of Lord Acton that power used to corrupt; in the wonder that is Independent India, corruption often empowers.

VIP Revolutionaries or When Revolution Is a Bottle of Scotch

Once upon a time, every intellectual in India was a Leftist — and every Leftist could pass off as an intellectual. The Berlin Wall came down; the Soviet Union collapsed; at home, the economy was opened up; liberalization, privatization, and market-friendliness became buzzwords. Many people were jubilant that socialism was out — bag and baggage. And since the Leftist intellectual was part of the baggage, he too would soon become a fossil. Or so it seemed.

But Leftist intellectuals have not only survived, they thrived; they are not only the fittest but also the shrewdest. And this was evident from the composition of the first Prasar Bharti Board which was filled with mostly Left-of-the-Centre intellectuals like historian Romila Thapar, journalist Nikhil Chakraborty, and Hindi writer Rajendra Yadav.

Earlier, it was fashionable to make statements like "I am a communist, not a gentleman." (These were the words of former West Bengal minister Ashok Mitra, who is fond of pontificating about socialism, social justice, and democracy in the newspapers owned by capitalists) Even as late as in 1997, the Chief Executive Officer of Prasar Bharti Corporation, SS Gill, had no compunction in saying that he was an "unrepentant Marxist," as he told a correspondent of *India Today*. But, generally, these days it is better to be a Left-liberal (L-l) or Left-of-the-Centre intellectual rather than a communist.

For one, if you are an L-l intellectual, you don't have to give any explanations. Nobody would taunt you by saying, "But comrade, Pol Pot was also a communist." Or by reminding you that 80 million to 100 million people died under various communist regimes all over the world, as documented by an institute based in Paris. Nobody would be able to lambaste you by pointing out that if anybody could beat Hitler in barbarity and ruthlessness, it would only be Stalin, Mao, and Pol Pot; for all these people, millions of deaths were no more than statistics. Nobody would tease you about the Gulag, about the suppression of creative voices, about the thought police which tried to chain the minds of people. In short, if you are an L-1 intellectual, you are free from the burden of ideology. You are not a card-holder; so, you don't have to justify each and every action of the party. You are just an L-1 intellectual; you want to make the world a better place; and in this venture, you feel, there is a lot to be learnt from Marx. You don't believe that the events in the erstwhile Soviet Union and China have discredited Marxism. You ardently believe some socio-political philosophy inspired from Marx, minus its sanguinary collectivization drives, labor camps, and Gulags, is still possible; purges and slave camps are not the integral parts of Marxism. There is Marxism beyond Soviet Union and Mao. Or one can still learn from the humanism of Marx.

Further, being an L-1 intellectual is politically correct, socially respectable, and economically lucrative. The L-1 intellectual has the license to earn and spend as much as he can. (If others do the same, they are the filthy rich, noveau riche, sunk in crude and crass consumerism, insensitive to the plight of the suffering humanity, etc). He could be leading or participating in a human rights outfit; he could be running a non-government organization (NGO). He receives huge amounts from government and foreign agencies. The L-1 intellectual does not see any anomaly or inconsistency in taking money from the government which, in his view, is a class institution whose *raison d'etre* is to keep the subalterns in bondage. Nor does he feel any qualms about receiving money from foreign bodies. When pumped into the outfits run by L-1 intellectuals — and invested in the state run by Marxists, West Bengal — foreign money is not bad; but normally, it is very bad. Multinationals, in particular, are the agents of Satan. With their resources and clout, they are the harbingers of neo-imperialism. Remember what they did in Iran and Chile? And remember East India Company?

Another benefit of being an L-1 intellectual is that one can become an authority on anything. One could be living in the US, but one could always philosophize about the poverty in India. One could be based in Europe, but one would be able to write on the idea of India. We must admit that this benefit is not exclusive to L-1 intellectuals; even card-holding members of the communist party enjoy this. But yes, objectivity is indeed a prerogative of every Leftist. An illustration: even if you are a card-holding member of the CPI or the CPM, your ideological-political affiliation will in no way cast its shadow on your work; in the intellectual circles, you won't be seen as biased or prejudiced. But, on the other hand, if you say at some point that the country should go for the uniform civil code, as it is also mentioned in the Constitution — or even if you say something as innocuous as that the BJP stand on this or that particular issue is reasonable — immediately you would be branded as a knickerwallah. Even if you have never attended any *shakha* of the RSS, never been a member of any of the organizations of the Sangh *parivar*, or never have voted for the BJP. Even if you are able to convince the intellectuals about your non-RSS background, you would be targeted as a "closet Nazi", or as one who wears knickers under one's trousers?

On the other hand, if you are an L-1 intellectual you possess all that is virtuous, noble, and exalted in the universe; you are good against bad, secular against communal, progressive against regressive, enlightened against obscurantist, right against the Right, and long goes the list. Many L-1 intellectuals have spent their lives in combating American imperialism in the agreeable surroundings of university campuses and air-conditioned seminar rooms; but nobody could dare to accuse them of reneging on their earlier stand when they end up becoming supporters of the nuclear imperialism of the US. So, the well-known journalist, Praful Bidwai, has no compunction in arguing the case that India should sign the comprehensive test ban treaty (CTBT), though he is also a vociferous opponent of the World Trade Organization (WTO). The WTO is for the benefit of developed countries, but the CTBT is for disarmament. Or so goes the argument. Similarly, former Prime Minister Chandra Shekhar read out in Parliament a letter Bhabani Sengupta had written to an American newspaper in the wake of the Pokhran nuclear explosion. Sengupta, a prominent Leftist intellectual, had argued in the letter that it would be futile for the US to impose sanctions against India because they won't work. But he was not opposed to the idea of sanctions against his own country. What is conspicuous is the fact that even after this expose, Sengupta did not show any shame or guilt for the anti-national views he had aired in 1974 in a foreign country; indeed, he demonstrated remarkable self-righteousness, obstinacy, and recalcitrance. The Bidwais and the Senguptas can never be castigated for two reasons: first, these honorable men — being the sole repositories of wisdom and morality — are above reproach; second, they can always claim that they are promoting disarmament, international harmony, etc. They are also peace-loving against jingoism (that is how patriotism is known in Leftist circles).

Where do all these worthies come from? Raj Thapar, in her book *All These Years,* has described the intellectual climate of the forties as follows:

> Marxism was constantly quoted, how accurately, I could not tell, and what never seemed to occur in the midst of frenzied arguments was the obvious incongruity of holding a juicy job in a foreign firm on the one hand and entertaining ideas of communism on the other. Accusations of being a Menshevik or a Bolshevik, of being a reactionary or a progressive could be hurled from a *boxwallah* to an independent. . . without a shade of guilt or absurdity. . . . The communists. . . . were as much part of the social elite of Bombay at the time as anyone else.

Even today, like SS Gill, a former IAS officer, one can be part of the most elitist service and remain an "unrepentant Marxist"! After retirement, one can still head a huge organization (Prasar Bharti Corporation) in a bourgeois system and treat it as his fiefdom — as Gill pompously thundered in an interview: "I have to decide."

Hari Shankar Parsai, an eminent Hindi satirist who was also a Marxist, classified Indian radicals into two categories:

> There is an Ordinary Revolutionary who organizes the masses. He starves, gets bashed up, goes to jail. . . . Then there is an

ultra-revolutionary, the VIP Revolutionary. During the day, he trims his beard, sits in the coffee house, sips the bitter coffee. . . . He violently stubs the cigarettes as if he were battering the bourgeoisie. He crams up the revolutionary quotes of Marx, Lenin, and Mao. At night, he boozes with his friends and mouths those revolutionary quotes. Then he attacks the chicken as if he were mauling capitalism.

For such "revolutionaries," added Parsai, "discussion is a luxury, slogan are good entertainment, and revolutionism is another bottle of Scotch."

That was in the 1970s. Most of the L-l intellectuals of today are the descendants of the VIP Revolutionary. Earlier, the Ordinary Revolutionary would organize movements of the subalterns — and face the consequences; the VIP Revolutionary would organize protest marches in the Capital against state repression; or, still better, would go to America on fellowship to write books on such movements. L-l intellectuals still write books on similar subjects.

The most interesting thing about L-l intellectuals is that they want to be known as anti-Establishment radicals, though the fact is that they are very much part of the Establishment. It is not only the Prasar Bharti Board that they man but also other countless government-aided bodies. They are involved in the writing of textbooks, setting norms in the fields of art, culture, 'art' cinema, and literature. It is, however, not clear whether what they indulge in is deception or self-deception.

Summary

In India, the Left is often seen as synonymous with communism. Perhaps, one reason for this is that the dominance of communists in the Left Front. Another, more important, reason is that socialism is a widely used term in our country, as in the wide world. Moreover, the adherents of Indian socialism have united and divided endlessly. Unlike the communists, they have also merged their identity with various parties and coalitions, e.g. in the Janata Party in 1977 and the Janata Dal in 1989. It won't be an exaggeration to say that socialists — along with their idiosyncrasies and, if any, ideology — have dissipated in Indian politics. In a similar manner as Leftist ideas have permeated the various human rights groups and non-governmental organizations, especially after the global decline of communism.

Such dissipation and permeation has created a motley pink group. It comprises people from various walks of life: Left-of-the-Centre academics and intellectuals who put caste, gender, etc., before class; civil liberty activists who often appear to be the frontmen of terrorists; green fanatics whose world is inhabited only by tribals and traditional communities; aristocratic socialists who are most prominent in denouncing nuclear blasts; the illuminati who crusade against Western or American imperialism — and go to a Western university; teenybopper intellectuals who are most likely to say, "Oh, Diana was so cute" and "Mother Teresa was full of compassion."

Epilogue

Roots of Rootlessness

We have elsewhere discussed the rootlessness of Indian communists. We have also discussed the push and pull factors. But without a brief study of modernity, the rootlessness of communists cannot be put into perspective.

The modern age bears the mark of the "Enlightenment project." The eighteenth century Enlightenment in Europe was leavened by the ideas of humanism, rationalism, and progress. "The empiricists of the eighteenth century, impressed by the vast new realms of knowledge opened by the natural sciences based on mathematical techniques, which had driven out so much error, superstition, dogmatic nonsense, asked themselves, like Socrates, why the same methods should not succeed in establishing similar irrefutable laws in the realm of human affairs. With the new methods discovered by natural science, order could be introduced into the social sphere as well," writes Isaiah Berlin, a contemporary philosopher, in *The Crooked Timber of Modernity* (1991). "The rational reorganization of society would put an end to spiritual and intellectual confusion, the reign of prejudice and superstition, blind obedience to unexamined dogmas, and the stupidities and cruelties of the oppressive regimes which such intellectual darkness bred and promoted. All that was wanted was the identification of the principal human needs and discovery of the means to satisfy them."

Reason was the means required, and the society and the polity guided by reason would "put an end to spiritual and intellectual confusion, the reign of prejudice. . . ." Not surprisingly, the eighteenth century is also known as the Age of Reason. In this age, writes Oxford scholar David Harvey in *The Condition of Postmodernity*, thinkers "took it as axiomatic that there was only one possible answer to any question. From this it followed that the world could be controlled and rationally ordered if we could only picture and represent it rightly. But this presumed that there existed a single correct way of representation which, if we could uncover it (and this was what scientific and mathematical endeavors were all about), would provide means to Enlightenment ends." In short, the Enlightenment was a belief in "linear progress, absolute truths, and rational planning of ideal social orders."

When this Enlightenment project reached the shores of India along with British imperialism, an unprecedented situation arose. For the first time, India and the West found each other face to face, what followed was an interaction which had far-reaching and profound consequences for Indian civilization. Not that the Indian and European civilizations were stranger to each other. Megasthenes had stayed at the court of the Mauryas in the third century BC (and is, in fact, an important source of information about that period). Trade between India and Rome flourished for centuries. Even during the medieval period, contacts between India and the West did not dry up; many travelers visited India.

However, there was a qualitative difference between the earlier contacts and those which followed when the British established their empire in our country. For, their empire was not to be sustained by the force of arms only; they also needed a class of Indians who would man the different bodies of the government and act as a medium, a buffer zone between the imperial rulers and the natives. So, the British created a class who were "Indian in blood and color, but British in taste, in opinion, in morals, and in intellect," as Macaulay put it in 1835.

Macaulay's dream was realized, but not exactly as he had desired. The people who were educated in the British system not only acquired the basic skills to become part of imperial administration but also got acquainted with Western humanism and rationalism, Voltaire and Rousseau, Bentham and Mill. But, at the same time, the Westernizing influence was not uniform on all Indians. There were some sections, like the Derozians in Bengal, who were overwhelmed by the West; and there were also people like the Arya Samajis who, while conceding Europe's superiority in science and technology, felt that India was second to none in past achievements, potentials, and matters pertaining to spirituality.

Such was the socio-cultural background of the intelligentsia when communist ideas started spreading in India. Here the position of communists in the modern era has to be seen in proper perspective. Communism is a proud child of modernism — though its adversaries charge, not without evidence, that more often than not it has tried to crush the ideals of humanism and rationalism (A report was recently brought out by a Paris-based organization that 80 to 100 million people perished under various communist regimes). Yet, communism is a dogmatically consistent product of modernism. It completely dispenses with the past, traditions, and conventions. It is a complete philosophy, an ideology that explains everything under the sun and beyond it; it is a concretized world view, a *weltanschauung*. It wants "end to spiritual and intellectual confusion, the reign of prejudice and superstition, blind obedience to unexamined dogmas, and the stupidities and cruelties of the oppressive regimes which such intellectual darkness bred and promoted."

So, in a communist system everything — the polity, the economy, the society, arts, culture, literature, cinema — is sought to be "controlled and rationally ordered." Further, as there is "only one possible answer to any question," any alternative understanding or suggestion to that of the party line is nothing short of blasphemy. It is likewise dealt with, the

Gulag being a grim reminder of the horrors of "the rational reorganization of society."

In the Indian context, when the deracinating elements of Western education came into contact with the monism of the Red variety, the effect was synergistic: the communist leader was a thoroughly rootless creature. Any politician who has faith in some ideals sometimes gets carried by them. However, if he is totally bewitched by them, he loses sight of the reality. For Indian communists, the bewitchment was a state of mind — at least, till the eighties.

A consequence of this bewitchment was self-righteousness and intellectual arrogance. Indian communists are always sure of the correctness of what they say or do. The other viewpoint does not deserve to exist. Just notice the arrogance and sanguineness of Indrajit Gupta, AB Bardhan, Jyoti Basu, and HS Surjeet when they appear on television; even when they are insisting on a very stupid point, they are supremely confident about their stand. The kind of language that top leaders of the CPM used for the prime minister and the home minister of the BJP government in 1998 was, to put it mildly, uncouth and uncivilized. This was when the Central government had sent a team to review the law and order situation in West Bengal. Similarly, in the aftermath of Pokhran-II, West Bengal Chief Minister Jyoti Basu had the temerity to criticize the BJP government in London on its nuclear policy — which was not just a breach of protocol but also anti-national. And we are discussing the things in the post-Soviet era — when the demolition of the Berlin Wall and Lenin's statues had shaken most comrades, and postmodern theories had dismissed Marxism as a metanarrative. In the good old days — when the communists claimed to possess the map of a new world, and their claims were taken quite seriously — there was absolutely no question of the validity of any other viewpoint. Least of a viewpoint rooted in the traditions, values, or culture of India; indeed, any such thing was seen with suspicion and contempt.

Why Did the Left Fail in India?

Has the Left failed in India? On the face of it, the answer seems to be in the negative. It was because of the influence of the Left that as early as in 1931 a resolution on fundamental rights and economic policy was passed at the Karachi session of the Congress. It stated, "The State shall own or control key industries and services, mineral resources, railways, waterways, shipping and other means of public transport." Socialist tenets are also reflected in several Directive Principles of the Constitution. After Independence, it was a socialist, Jawaharlal Nehru, who presided over the affairs of the country. And he tried to translate his ideas into reality; the Planning Commission and public sector units bear testimony to his sincerity.

Besides, the word 'Leftist' is considered synonymous with "intellectual." As discussed elsewhere, Leftist influence on the intellectual class is, to put it mildly, tremendous; some call it a sort of strangulation, asphyxiation, etc. Leftists have indeed flourished in this country, but the principal Leftist goals — empowerment of the poor, uplift of the downtrodden, fulfillment of the basic needs of the dispossessed — have been anything but attained. After 50 years of independence, decades of socialist planning, and spending billions of rupees, poverty is conspicuous by it starkness. P Sainath, in his book *Everybody Loves a Good Drought*, has given poignant examples of penury, misery, and wretchedness prevalent all over the country: the tapper of date-palm jaggery in Ramnad district, Tamil Nadu, has to climb tall palm trees 150 times to earn Rs 5-8; the allotment of non-existent plots to the landless in Palamu, Bihar; a short, frail woman in Dodda, Bihar, has to carry 40 kg on her head twice from her village to the *haat* (local market) to make her both ends meet; uprooted tribals and their miserable plight. Of course, one need not read Sainath's book to know about poverty in the country; one just has to see around oneself. In a country where every third person lives below the poverty line, only an incorrigible worshipper of Nehru would claim that socialism has succeeded.

We shall study the failure of the Left in two parts: first, failure of Indian socialism; and, second, the failure of Indian communism. The former we have already discussed in a chapter. Here we try to find out why communists could not take over the reins.

Every educated Indian imbibed the Western values of humanism, rationalism, and liberalism in varying measures. But some of them did that fanatically; they became completely Westernized in taste, opinion, intellect, and morals. Such people belonged to a unique class. Most of the communist leaders came from this class. They came from well-to-do families. They came into contact with Marxian ideas in Western universities, where being a Leftist had become a fad. Bright young men as they were, they found Gandhi's methods ineffective and his ideology regressive. And this was the product and function of the conditions prevalent in India which was a backward country with people who were illiterate, superstitious, religious, and caste-ridden. The ray of hope had to come from the West. In other words, there was a push factor (a benighted nation with no worthwhile leadership or progressive values to speak of) and a pull factor (Marxism). This is how the brown sahibs became communists.

Of course, there were a number of other leaders who were thoroughly Westernized. Arguably, Jawahalal Nehru was the most prominent among them. He was also influenced by Karl Marx. So, how was he different from communists? He has been called an incorrigible idealist, a dreamer; for these reasons, he greatly harmed national interests — e.g., in the Kashmir affair and *vis-à-vis* China; yet, even his worst detractors don't call him a traitor, a charge which is often hurled at Indian communists. There are two reasons for it. One, in spite of all his fascination for the West and Marxian philosophy, he never accepted the latter as a dogma. Second, though his views about the Indian nation were at variance with those of the Hindutva ideologue, Savarkar, he never denied its existence; he acknowledged the fact that India as a nation had had thousands of years of history, whereas for our comrades India was no more than "a geographical expression".

Ignoring the reality of Indian nation, and consequently of national sentiments, cost Indian communists dearly. In fact, wherever in the world communism succeeded, it was because of its alliance with nationalism; both blended so well that they became indistinguishable from each other. For, what people identify themselves with and die for is the nation, the country, the motherland, the fatherland; for something as abstract as ideology only commissars can sacrifice their, and others' lives. People ardently and passionately defend their land, as they did when the enemies of the Bolshevik Revolution attacked Russia with the help of Western countries. For the Russian masses what was at stake was, besides their newly-gained land rights, the independence of their country. So, the Bolsheviks were as much fighting for Russia as for Marxism. When Hitler attacked Russia in 1941, the hitherto "imperialist war" might have metamorphosed into a "people's war" for Indian communists, but for the Russians it became the Great Patriotic War, the Great Fatherland War, and the National War of Liberation. According to *Encyclopedia Britannica*, during the Second Word War, "the reservoirs of patriotic sacrifice on which the [Soviet] regime was able to draw helped to ensure its survival".

> Stalin, in his first broadcast to the nation on 3 July 1941, was wise enough to identify himself with this patriotic upsurge and to exploit it to the full. . . . The cult of Stalin fused with the new patriotism. Slogans of class struggle were put aside, at least temporarily. Anti-religious propaganda was subdued, church leaders were wooed, and the patriachate was restored, and the church faithful joined in defence of their country. A new anthem replaced the "Internationale." The Army was glorified, and patriotic songs dominated the mass media. The nationalist revival that Stalin led was an important key to victory. . . .

Similarly, Chinese communists were also in the forefront of the Japanese imperialists. Edgar Snow writes in *The Other Side of the River*, "China's outstanding communists were internationalist in ideology but no less national patriots than the Kuomintang 'nationalists'."

In Cuba, too, what rallied the entire country behind Fidel Castro was the persistent attempts by the United States to dislodge him by hook or by crook. This is not to say that his charismatic leadership and socio-economic reforms he initiated played no role in the consolidation of his regime, but the American conspiracies were also quite significant. The legendary revolutionary leader, Che Guevara, in a secret meeting with an American official, actually thanked him for the Bay of Pigs invasion the US had planned. This invasion, the revolutionary told the official, had made every Cuban a Castro supporter. Interestingly, Castro was not even a communist at the time of the Cuban revolution in 1959; it was only later that he became one and an ally of the Soviet Union.

The story of the Vietnam War is also not much different. It was essentially a nationalist struggle which the Americans mistook for a communist uprising. Here too, the communists were "internationalist in ideology" but "national patriots" in practice.

Indian communists were, however, internationalist in ideology as well as practice — and internationalist to a fault. For them, nationalism was, and is, anathema. Not only did they little to establish their nationalist credentials, they were often sympathetic to the enemy — with the British in 1942, with the Muslim League in 1947, with the Chinese in 1962. This was as much against patriotic feeling as against common sense. For, treason is something all self-respecting peoples loath. Major Quisling was a Norwegian who collaborated with Hitler; today, the word "Quisling" is synonymous with traitor. Similarly, nearer home, Vibhishana helped Lord Ram, the *Maryadapurushottam* (the one who embodies all that is virtuous, just, and good) against Ravana, who epitomized evil and arrogance. Yet, Vibhishan is denigrated, even by the worshippers of Ram. As they say, *ghar ka bhedi Lanka dhaye* — the traitor causes doom. For their anti-Indian and anti-national views, Indian communists were not fully trusted by the people.

In this context, a mention of Naxalites is pertinent. They were extremists in the true sense of the word — in practice as well in theory. They even declared their allegiance to the Chinese leadership. A Naxalite leader went to Beijing and met Premier Chou En-lai and Kang Sheng, member of the Standing Committee of the politburo of the Communist Party of China. He probably also met Mao Tse-tung. Kang lambasted the Naxalites for their slogan, "China's chairman is our chairman." This slogan was coined by Charu Mazumdar, one of the pioneers and preeminent leaders of the Naxalite movement. Kang said, "We don't agree with your calling our chairman your chairman. This is against principle and Mao Tse-tung's thought. Our relation is fraternal and equal." Chou was more forthcoming: "The world is divided into classes and nations. The proletariat of each territory is the chief representative of its own country. So, we cannot but take into consideration the national limits. To refer to the leader of our country as the leader of another party is against the sentiments of the nation. To respect a great Marxist-Leninist is one thing; but to declare him as one's leader is a different matter. It is a question of principle." Chou also added that "your path can be worked out only by you."

In other words, Chinese leaders gave a lesson of patriotism to an Indian Marxist! Foreigners told him not to go "against the sentiments of the nation!" Could there be anything more comic? Interestingly, the Chinese leaders were just evoking the thoughts of Satyabhakta, the founder of the Indian Communist Party, but now a forgotten figure in the history of the Left.

Another important factor for the failure of communism was the Indian National Congress. There was no liberal opinion or organization in Russia, China, Cuba, or Vietnam. The peculiar and extreme conditions in each of these countries stunted the growth of liberalism in these countries. In India, however, the Congress was not only the strongest political body but was also inclusivist in nature — accommodating various classes, creeds, interests, even ideologies.

Indian communists' indifferent attitude towards the peasantry is another reason for their limited political strength in the country. Till the Chinese Revolution in 1949, there was hardly any serious effort to involve the rural masses, the CPI endeavor in organizing the Workers' and Peasants' Parties in various parts of the country notwithstanding. This was because they dogmatically followed Marx, Engels, and Lenin. In the *Manifesto of the Communist Party* (1848), Marx and Engels wrote, "They [peasants] are. . . not revolutionary but conservative. Nay, more, they are reactionary, for they want to roll back the wheel of history." The bourgeoisie had saved a considerable portion of population from "the idiocy of rural life." In their later years, the duo somewhat revised their views about the role of the peasantry. In the preface of *The Peasant War in Germany* (1870), Engels wrote, "The day the farm laborers learned to understand their own interests, a reactionary, feudal, bureaucratic, or bourgeois government became impossible in Germany." Once again, in 1894, Engels spoke about the collaboration between the peasantry and the proletariat, this time in the context of France. Yet, the peasantry was seen as a passive supporter rather than the vanguard of the revolution.

Lenin, too, had made it amply clear much before the Bolshevik Revolution that the proletariat would play the predominant role. In January 1905, he wrote, "Our struggle for the revolution, our preparation for the revolution, will be at the same time an unsparing struggle with liberalism for influence over the masses, for the leading role of the proletariat in the revolution." Again he wrote in October 1905, "The complete victory of the revolution means the victory of the proletariat."

However, what the Indian communists failed to recognize was the fact that Lenin and his comrades were too pragmatic and realistic to ignore the interests of the peasantry — and this proved crucial. Peasants at once became supporters of the Bolsheviks when the latter gave the slogan "Land to the tiller." On the other hand, no Indian communist of any consequence saw great revolutionary potential in peasants. For instance, BT Ranadive ardently supported the Telengana movement. He said, "Telengana today means communists and communists mean

Telengana" (1948). He even hoped that Telengana would become the Yunan of India; revolution would spread from here to all parts of the country, as it did in China. Yet, he was of the opinion that "the agrarian revolution must be championed by the working class." And throughout his life, Ranadive remained active in the trade union movement.

And whenever and wherever the communists have championed their interests in India, the Red flag has made deep inroads. West Bengal is the best example: one of the main reasons why the CPI(M) has been able to rule continuously for more than two decades in this state is the land reforms they carried under Operation Barga. In the pockets of Bihar and Andhra Pradesh, too, the communists have a strong presence mainly because of their espousal of the cause of small farmers and agricultural laborers.

Even on the industrial front, Indian communists have failed to evolve a distinct revolutionary ethos, an alternative industrial vision, or a novel work culture among the masses where they are powerful. Reacting to the West Bengal governor's address at the opening of the Budget session in 1984, Partha Chatterjee wrote in *Frontier* (3 March 1984): "The centre has been blamed for its tardiness in granting licenses for three major industrial projects in the public sector. Yet the speech does nothing to rectify what has been obvious for quite some time — that the Left Front does not have an industrial policy at all. It has talked from time to time of helping small capitalists in the private sector but, unlike other states in southern or western India, has been unable to clarify its political position sufficiently in order to actively promote capitalist development of this sort. On the other hand, it has made itself more dependent on the aid from international funding agencies in order to run its infrastructural programmes, particularly in the metropolitan areas. The performance of its own public sector units is abysmal, to the extent that it has had to make an offer, unprecedented in India, to private capitalists to take back some of the units now languishing in the nationalized sector. The Left Front's policy on industry has been one of complete ad hocism. It has constantly acceded to the power of the organized interests and thus sought to drift along the path of least resistance."

It couldn't have been otherwise. For, "the organized interests" — unionized workers, government employees — have played a key role in the rise of the Left in West Bengal. They are an integral part of the middle class which — thanks to its brahmanical contempt for business — has never been favorably disposed towards industry, trade, and commerce. They vote for the Left Front and attend all their programs and rallies. In the past, they never faced any moral qualms when they de-industrialized West Bengal; nor do they suffer any pricks of conscience when they go for three-hour-long lunches and one-hour-long tea-breaks.

In general, the problem with the Left is that it has failed to provide an exemplar. It has all along been vociferously championing the cause of the public sector; but it has not been able to run PSUs efficiently; some of them were handed over to the private sector.

Owing to their dogmatic approach, communists were not very successful in India. And wherever they were successful, as in West Bengal and Kerala, their performance has been as good or as bad as of the others.

Bankruptcy of the Right (1)

In this book, an effort has been made to study the hegemony and influence of the Left. The intellectual bankruptcy and moral hollowness of Leftists have been widely discussed. We have also mentioned the lack of social and economic content in the post-independence Rightist agenda; and this, we maintain, has helped in the intellectual ascendance of the Left (See "Intellectual Hegemony of the Left"). But the Right's problem is much more severe: what it suffers from is downright cerebral poverty.

Here we shall discuss only the Bharatiya Janata Party (BJP), as there is no other political party that is known as Rightist. Long back, there was a Rightwing group, the Swatantra Party, which represented the interests of feudal elements and big business and championed the cause of *laissez faire* when socialism was fashionable; it was the economic Right, whereas the BJP's predecessor, Bharatiya Jana Sangha (JS), was seen as the religious Right. By the mid-seventies, Swatantra Party had become a spent force.

But is the BJP Rightwing? Generally, Rightwing groups are those which lay more emphasis on continuity than on change; to them change sans continuity is anathema. For a Rightwinger, a society is more than the sum total of individuals; it is also a repository of values, traditions, and culture, each of which is indispensable for the nation. The *Encyclopedia Britannica* succinctly summarizes two characteristics of conservatism: "a distrust of human nature, of rootlessness, of untested innovations; and a corresponding trust in unbroken historical continuity and in traditional frameworks within which human affairs may be conducted."

In the Indian context, "unbroken historical continuity" is difficult to find. There have been at least two major discontinuities in the history of India — the coming of Muslims in the thirteenth century and of the British at the fag end of the eighteenth century. Leftists don't consider the first one as a major discontinuity — that is, if they view the arrival of Muslims as a discontinuity at all. For Hindu nationalists, however, the conquest of India by Muslims was the worst tragedy the country has ever suffered; the Muslim era, they say, was marked by decline, decadence, intolerance, barbarism, vandalism, massacres, plunder, and forced conversion. British rule, too, has been seen as exploitative, brutal, repressive, and a factor in the dismemberment of the motherland in 1947. India would have been a better place without these discontinuities.

The problem with Hindu nationalists' philosophy of history is that it does not take into account the impact of these two discontinuities. Here it must be noted that India is the only country in the world where Muslims ruled for more than five centuries, and yet it did not become Muslim. Though Hindus retained their identity under Muslim rule, their society, culture, philosophy, and values underwent profound changes. The same with British rule; in fact, it was under the British influence in the nineteenth century that self-awareness dawned upon Hindus. But this awareness was also tinged with Macaulayan imperatives. The early nationalists saw India through the eyes of the West. Many realities were recognized; but quite a few fictions were also created, mainly to instill national consciousness among the people. The most prominent of them was the Indian spiritualism-Western materialism dichotomy.

In the twenties of the twentieth century, when Mahatma Gandhi took over the reins of the national movement, Indian nationalism assumed a trajectory that earlier leaders like Lokmanya Tilak and Lala Lajpat Rai would have deprecated: it became divorced from Hinduism. Cut off from the mainstream, Hindu nationalism languished intellectually as well as politically. It was caught in a vicious circle: it could not grow as a vibrant political philosophy because it could not attract people with heightened consciousness; and it could not attract such people because they found little vibrancy in it.

As a consequence, Hindu nationalism fell prey to the retrograde, ill-informed elements, whose perception of India was a melange of the nineteenth century fictions and downright ignorance. For them, India was the fountainhead of all that is noble, glorious, and benevolent in mankind. All sciences emanated from our country; our literature, philosophy, arts, culture are the best in the world; our society is the most tolerant and humane; our values are sublime. Such things are heard even in the last decade of the second millennium. The RSS, the Shiv Sena, the Vishwa Hindu Parishad, and the Bajrang Dal are full of worthies who believe, as a third-rate Hindi film song says, "East or the West, India is the best."

As Hindu nationalism was depleted of substance and vibrancy over the years, dependence on a supposedly golden past grew proportionately. The ascendance of backward-looking, semi-educated people was a concomitant development. They knew little about the past of their own country; the past, in their scheme of things, was glorious because it was remote, at a far-

off point in the space-time continuum where there were
enlightened sages and wise seers, the Vedas and the
Upanishadas, the land of milk and honey, an idyllic Utopia we
all should strive to bring back on earth. Such people can't be
expected to be even aware of the traditions, culture, values, and
essence of Hinduism. Nor could they be expected to conduct
human affairs "in traditional frameworks".

Yet, such elements played an important role in Hindu
resurgence in the eighties and nineties. They were best equipped
— because of their zealotry and narrow-mindedness — to fight
the anti-Hindu fanaticism of Leftist intellectuals and Muslim
fundamentalists. Leftist intellectuals would not listen to reason
while denigrating Hinduism or promoting an anti-Hindu cause;
the same with Islamic fanatics. Hindu nationalists also showed
remarkable disdain for reason. One kind of stupidity fought, and
demolished, another kind of stupidity. One of the consequences
was 6 December 1992.

Bankruptcy of the Right (2)

The problem with Hindu nationalism is that it could not grow
intellectually despite tremendous political growth. It could not
develop a worldview in tune with the modern world. Hindu
nationalist views about society, polity, history, culture, and
economics remained puerile at best and retrograde at worst.

To begin with, the BJP can hardly be called the economic
Right; in fact, the party often seems to be at odds with the latter.
The foremost champions of the economic Right are people who
are often accused of being unduly influenced, if not exactly
sponsored, by the World Bank, the IMF, and the US. They are
opposed to socialism, the public sector, government controls,
subsidies, etc, and favor free enterprise, privatization,
globalization, decontrol, etc. But these people have no
compunctions in condemning the supposedly Rightwing BJP on
matters like the Ramjanmabhoomi Temple and nuclear blasts.
On such questions, the economic Right just echoes the views of
Leftwing and teeny-bopper intellectuals.

As for the economic policy of the BJP, it is no more than a mixture of wishful thinking and fashionable fads. It might be argued that though the BJP — or the JS earlier — has never been a supporter of socialism, it has never completely ignored the economic realities. For instance, the 1951 manifesto of the JS says:

> The most important economic problem before the country today is that of food, clothing and shelter. . . . In the interest of the economy of the country the party would abolish Jagirdari and Zamindari as with compensation and distribute the land to tillers. . . . The party stands for public ownership of industries especially catering to the essential defence needs of the country. . . . Effective steps will be taken to put a check on profiteering and concentration of economic power in the hands of the big few through cartels and combines. . . . The party stands for a fair deal to labor. . . . The taxation policy would be so directed that it lessens inequalities of income.

Could a social democratic party have said something fundamentally different from what the JS was saying in 1951? Or what it said in its 1954 manifesto? It declared: "For increasing production and reconstructing rural society, Jana Sangha will *radically* reform the land system. All land belongs to Society" (emphasis added). In their later manifestoes, too, the BJS and the BJP showed remarkable concern for the pressing social and economic issues.

However, in India party manifestos are just an exercise in pomposity; during elections, every party brings out — for the sake of convention rather than for the benefit of voters — a few pages of magnificent nonsense. What matters in elections are emotive issues and smart slogans like *Garibi Hatao*, not manifestoes. Few read manifestos; fewer, if any, take them seriously. Not surprisingly, manifestoes of most parties say the same or similar things on most issues. It is the emphasis which parties lay on different issues that makes them different. And people come to know of the emphasis from the statements of leaders, the programs the parties launch, and the stand they take on crucial matters. For instance, in late 1990, both the Janata Dal and the BJP were *technically* committed to the implementation of the Mandal Commission Report and the building of the Ram temple; it was the difference of emphasis that made the two parties different. The Janata Dal came to be known as pro-Mandal and anti-Mandir, and the BJP as pro-Mandir and anti-Mandal.

The emphasis of the BJP has seldom been on economic questions; there have been knee-jerk reactions on matters pertaining to economy, never an economic philosophy. At times, it speaks of curiosities like Hindu economics, but it is doubtful if even BJP supporters take such esoteric gibberish seriously. What has really moved the BJP has always been issues like those of cow protection and Ram temple, the appeasement of Muslims and the infiltration by Bangladeshis. Whatever little the party has to say on unemployment, poverty alleviation, industrialization, etc, is so badly enmeshed in the Swadeshi jargon and time-worn shibboleths that one can't make out head or tail of it. The saffron mindset is undoubtedly medieval as far as economic affairs are concerned. They don't know what is really happening in the world. Ironically, they seem to be parroting the Leftist slogans regarding neo-imperialism and multinational corporations.

It is not only in the sphere of economic policies that the Right has shown monumental incompetence and scandalous duplicity but in other departments as well. When BJP leaders are running down the misdeeds and misrule of a Congress government, at the Centre or in any of the states, few can match them in cogency or eloquence. But when it comes to governance, the BJP has seldom shown excellence; in fact, the party has often failed to live up to its promises and performed poorly. Madhya Pradesh was lost, thanks to the inefficiency of Sunderlal Patwa. This despite the fact that the Congress, the only other major party in the state, has always been a divided house. In Maharashtra and Rajasthan, the performance of state governments was so bad that the electorate rejected the party in the 1998 general elections.

In Delhi state, too, where the BJP won six out of seven Lok Sabha seats in 1998, the party provided an administration which was, to put it mildly, callous and apathetic. The Capital was, and is, suffering from all kinds of problems one can think of — unemployment, pollution, lack or absence sanitation, scarcity of water and power, shoddy public transportation system, deteriorating law and order scene — you name a problem and it is there. But what the BJP mayor of Delhi, Shakuntala Arya, was concerned about was that the young people should not kiss in public parks! And what is the BJP style of tackling important issues? When the bloodthirsty Redline buses wrought havoc on the roads of Delhi, and people started feeling that the name was quite appropriate — the color of blood being red — former Chief Minister of Delhi Madan Lal Khurana came up with a brilliant idea: change the color of the buses from red to blue, and they would start behaving! His successor, Sahib Singh Verma, continued the tradition. A school bus fell into the Yamuna, leading to scores of casualties. Instead of taking a holistic view of the situation, preparing a comprehensive policy, and implementing it in all earnestness so that the commuting of school children becomes safer, Verma took a leaf out of Khurana's book and took recourse to political chromotherapy: he ordered that all school buses be painted yellow! The Delhi state government has taken any number of such absurd decisions, one of them being putting a ban on smoking at public places to check pollution. If aspirin could treat cancer, the BJP would have eradicated the deadly disease.

That the Right has not been able to propound or develop a proper, modern political philosophy is quite evident. It clearly can't boast of an Edmund Burke. The JS/BJP, along with a few others, have been quite right in pointing out the basic flaws of the Nehruvian model: socialism bred incompetence, bureaucratization, and corruption; secularism became an instrument to appease Muslims; foreign policy had no rational or national basis and little relation with common sense. But the BJP has not been able to provide a viable alternative in political theory: What kind of governance does it want to aspire to? What are the contours of the economic model it wants to project? How does it intend to tackle the problems of population, pollution, unemployment, etc? Would there be any breach with the past, in the sense that it would introduce a fundamentally different polity and economy if it is given an opportunity? All these and other similar questions draw a blank. Having failed to develop its own paradigm and idiom, the BJP was forced to conduct public discourse in the liberal-Marxian-Gandhian idiom. It was like fighting a duel with a weapon of the adversary's choice.

We have discussed elsewhere how Leftist historians and other scholars have propagated their politically- and ideologically-oriented doctrines; how truths, half-truths, and untruths have been amalgamated to justify such doctrines; how unsubstantiated theories pass off as self-evident truths. But, to their credit, at least the Leftists show respect to the scientific methodology; they are aware of what is happening in the world. They would rely on radio-carbon dating, if the antiquity of some object is to be determined. They have done thorough research in various aspects of their subject. DD Koshambi, for instance, did pioneering work in numismatics. The pro-BJP scholars, on the other hand, have confined themselves to proving that the Aryans were not outsiders, that the Taj Mahal was built by the Hindus, and similar kinky theories. In this context, it is not surprising that the intellectual class has little respect for the Right.

The same with the world of art and culture. True that the state has always supported the Left-of-the-Centre coterie; but lofty idealism and a vibrant ideology should be self-sustaining. The Indian Right did not provide any impetus to art and culture after independence. So, today saffron art critics are found only in the Bajrang Dal and the Vishwa Hindu Parishad who equate vandalism with art criticism and physical assault on artists with cultural discourse. Needless to say, obscurantism and medievalism have seldom attracted intellectuals anywhere in the world.

Not that the Sangh Parivar doesn't have its own "front organizations" to trumpet its cause; it has bodies like Sanskar Bharti. But, unlike communist front organizations like IPTA and Progressive Writers' Association, none of the saffron cultural outfits has been able to make any mark. The list of people associated with IPTA reads like the who's who of Indian theater. In the realm of Indian literature, too, the Leftists have carved a niche for themselves. But what has been the contribution of Sanskar Bharti? In fact, not many people in the world of art and culture have even heard its name.

In other words, Leftists never had serious competition in any sphere of life. They can be compared with a team who are lucky enough to bat on a ground where there are no fielders; any shot they hit goes to the fence.

Index